A N N E    W A L D M A N

# Helping the Dreamer

NEW & SELECTED POEMS 1966-1988

COFFEE HOUSE PRESS  ::  MINNEAPOLIS

Some of these poems appeared in the following books and pamphlets: BABY BREAKDOWN (Bobbs-Merrill), GIANT NIGHT (Corinth Books), FAST SPEAKING WOMAN (The Red Hanrahan Press and City Lights), SUN THE BLOND OUT (Arif), JOURNALS & DREAMS (Stonehill), CABIN (Z Press), FIRST BABY POEMS (Rocky Ledge Cottage Editions, Hyacinth Girls), MAKEUP ON EMPTY SPACE (Toothpaste Press), INVENTION (Kulchur Foundation), SKIN MEAT BONES (Coffee House Press). Poems in the final section of this book, *Helping the Dreamer*, appeared in the following magazines and anthologies: *Bombay Gin, Broadway, Conjunctions, Exquisite Corpse, Human Means, New Directions 52, Notus, Stiletto, The American Poetry Review, The City Lights Review, The Vajradhatu Sun, Tyuonyi*. Broadsides of "Romance," "Philosophia Perennis," "Ancient Song Rising," and "Colors" (under the title "Optimum Blue") were published by Casa Sin Nombre, Coffee House Press, Pentagram, and River City Portfolio, respectively. For contributing words to "Iovis Omnia Plena," I thank John Waldman, Red Grooms, Douglas Dunn, Ambrose Bye, James Laughlin, Brendan Ritcheson, and Dan Mage.

The publisher thanks the following organizations whose support helped make this book possible: The National Endowment for the Arts, a federal agency; The Jerome Foundation; and United Arts.

Coffee House Press books are distributed to trade by CONSORTIUM BOOK SALES AND DISTRIBUTION, 213 East Fourth Street, Saint Paul, Minnesota 55101. Our books are also available through all major library distributors and jobbers, and through most small press distributors, including Bookpeople, Bookslinger, Inland, Pacific Pipeline, and Small Press Distribution. For personal orders, catalogs or other information, write to:

COFFEE HOUSE PRESS
27 NORTH FOURTH STREET, SUITE 400, MINNEAPOLIS, MN 55401.

Library of Congress Cataloging in Publication Data

Waldman, Anne, 1945-
    Helping the dreamer : selected poems, 1966-1988 / Anne Waldman.
        p.   cm.
    ISBN 0-918273-50-1 : $9.95
    I. Title.
PS3573.A4215H4        1989
811'.54 — dc20                    89-15706
                                              CIP

# Contents

for Reed

    &

      for Ambrose

*"my face*
*constant to you!"*

— WILLIAM CARLOS WILLIAMS

# COLLEGE UNDER WATER

*"These vendetta women will not be put off"*

## After "Les Fleurs"

— Paul Eluard

I am 20 years old and holding on
Knowing I'm still young, I love you world

I am not 20 years old. My past is deaf, deaf

I dream a life of crystals and lie down in the grass

You think I'm crying; I don't
Don't hurt me — let me be

My eyes a strength the color of my wounds,
Love, what is the sun when it rains?

I tell you there are things as true as this story

When I close my eyes I kill you.

## College Under Water

Who are these women and offices
that control the will of the dead graduates?

They come to dinner like swimmers
assembling before a final race

Now coffins are lined up outside
where campus elms seize precedence over girls

Now offices are closed for the afternoon
in correspondence with the courts and the pool

Now because instructed the sky changes hands
shuffling wills that are transferred

to file cards behind locked doors
These vendetta women will not be put off

Now I write like this because
it could happen   My will weakens

Is there a choice? the alternative
lies on the other side of the poem.

## The Blue That Reminds Me
## of the Boat When She Left

Folds on your shirt lie like shadows
who hide me before she's leaving
You know she's leaving. The flag signals
us to mask and cross a plank so that
the transition will be easier, less visual
The sun has moved a bit and
sadness takes on new shapes
You say "Her shape sleeps in me and
the world explodes around her until
every atom resembles the match trick
she taught us last night"
We translated the dream before she left
then waited in the park by the dock
under shadows that were increasing
on your shirt as the sun grew feeble
Now she sends us postcards of sky & sea that say:
"I have had crazy dreams lately! Last night
I was dead and my skin was the color of this picture."

## The De Carlo Lots

1

You are parceled out over the post office
Letters arrive from Jonathan, Sasha
A season in Millville, New Jersey.

The voice is feedback and not insensitive
to moths as light            dispersed in spots
through this room. When I see the particles
who rations these waves for me?

Only that you might sit here unafraid
listening to the termites eat out the walls
and wonder how they do it        the stamina,
I mean the breeding

It was about the family he confided.
The effect this might have on them
could not be ignored, even as they slept

And when letters would arrive the next morning
after the bicycle, who was to say
where was her heart in all of this?

2

Mailbags under the porch.
A calm across the lake.

The family hurts me as I lounge about
these pine walls trying to read
A scratching in the wood prevents sobriety, or else
the knowledge of it ending with the itching never
subsided.

The letters are damp with use.
My fingers are moist.
Inkstains cover the tablecloth
that now resembles "black"

A song that will always have the same hold
on you is painful for me, you see, because
I never even knew it and have nothing to
counter your passion,     the energy
with which you embrace the other girl's radio

3
She is no longer of use to them
when they forsake the lake for the ocean

In fact, she's almost a hindrance, the
way she likes to "cut-up" everything,
keeps using up paper     writes letters
and they don't let her go anyway
All the way.

You're swimming nude in the ocean.
It's 2:00 AM. Some policemen will come
and ask you to go     gently
when they see how young you are

You will mount the stairs to the attic
of the house where you're staying
the "house of Lynn's aunt who is away,"
and you will be surprised to see her
there between two beds,     two boys
They are putting on their clothes when
she says no,     don't go

Dear Jon,    This is Atlantic City
I am thirteen years old     This is the
birthday of the song they're playing
when they interrupt us eight years later

4
We are saying goodbye to the inanimate objects.
They are mostly of wood.
Light seeps through these cracks,
as squirrels in winter
when the lady comes cleaning up
misses them under the bedsheets

6

I am trying to imagine the light in winter, not
being told        as squirrels, termites.
I am learning how they live from books.
We are writing "Ten Facts" in the city.

Light defines these cracks which are of wood
as you are "my only shape and substance"
or the voice is dispersed in outlines
of spots through the room.

A beam crashes the dials.
I am thinking now of all the little animals.


5
The family is livening up the house
with the radio      but she is not there
and is only told later
the pine was "rocking"

You are perhaps on a boat watching
the children watching the sunset from the pier
or else fishing by the sand-bar, adoring the heron
The boat is rocking.

She is rationing out her love, as waves
are sectioned out over the lake
disappearing into the land,
sending the energy home


She remembers the couple going over the dam
in the canoe. Strangers from Vineland, New Jersey.
A song attached to them immediately.

These are foreign waters foreign objects float upon.
They are large splinters of wood and resemble
the pieces of letters
I can't seem to get off to you, off the shore

6

The bicycle trip is arduous and not unlike
the energy it takes descending these steps daily
seeing if the mail has come at 9:30 AM.

The energy is parceled out into the day.
His legs are weak from making love.

The forces it takes licking the envelope in
Athens come at me as the sounds shaking
the foundations of the house they're tearing apart.
It is of pine.
Only the land is not yours    the rest you may carry away,
while a telephone number tells you all the particles

Sasha's letter is brief.
He tells me he is happier in the water than
any other place and hopes to live there forever.
A couple crashes over the dam a splinter away.


7

We are dwelling on the surface of
something explosive, though not unlikely
subdued
as the cracks are blocked up with tissue.
Light or fire. It's all the same to me.

Where were they going from the post office
when she asked, are you driving back?
From Atlantic City where the music is live
and we turn on the radio      trying to capture
those lost waves

A naked girl is swimming in her view.
I've come here year after year.
The family hurts me as I try to swim,
abandoning these walls of pine and
what they represent in terms of "destructibility"

All my friends are entering the lake for the last time
as the energy leaves my birthplace and returns
to the city in September.
We study leaves, the lifespan of termites.

8

A great blast splinters the shelf that
holds the radio  when the voice
reaches me a second away and embraces
the girl fishing from the rowboat.

The sun is setting across the shore.
This is about the family who lived there.

I write to Jonathan and Sasha about the fireworks,
as the last song is rationed into the night

8
The dials are lots and are as inanimate
as the ground we walk on
That is to say, not without life or
waverings in the soil

He was as young as the girls who surrounded
him and they used to watch him mounting the
attic steps, going,        as he said,   to pray

Outside, a calm across the lake.
A peace after the accident.
A break in the day where "demolition"
ruled their lives,
gradually governed their words        their sleep
as she worried about the effect
this might have on all of them.

She would never let the others touch him
or played the radio when he came.
He told her she had cut herself up in little pieces
equally rationed among them and might easily
go away and never return,
only referring to the songs to counter
the energy of the other girl's swimming or
recall the light seeping through the cracks.

He said "I am thirteen years old"
That was eight years ago, when the dials
spilled all over the page

9
You are allotted a childhood as wood
splinters right under your thumbs.

It's as quickly as that, seeing the
children put on their clothes again
asking you not to turn away, but
to look back upon the waves again,
to even touch their burning limbs

Letters will record this season even
if the radio doesn't

And the wood eats the dials right
out of the pine

I mean the stamina with which this
whole life span is devoured

The family forgets.
The girl rises from the water and
comes towards us on the shore.

I am picking up the pieces to send to you,
measuring the lots, the dreams by

1966

# BABY BREAKDOWN

*"O rapture & destr*

*O phantom brain what?"*

## How the Sestina (Yawn) Works

I opened this poem with a yawn
thinking how tired I am of revolution
the way it's presented on television
isn't exactly poetry
You could use some more methedrine
if you ask me personally

People should be treated personally
there's another yawn
here's some more methedrine
Thanks! Now about this revolution
What do you think? What is poetry?
Is it like television?

Now I get up and turn off the television
Whew! It was getting to me personally
I think it is like poetry
Yawn   it's 4 AM yawn   yawn
This new record is one big revolution
if you were listening you'd understand methedrine

isn't the greatest drug no not methedrine
it's no fun for watching television
You want to jump up have a revolution
about something that affects you personally
When you're busy and involved you never yawn
it's more like feeling, like energy, like poetry

I really like to write poetry
it's more fun than grass, acid, THC, methedrine
If I can't write I start to yawn
and it's time to sit back, watch television
see what's happening to me personally:
war, strike, starvation, revolution

This is a sample of my own revolution
taking the easy way out of poetry
I want it to hit you all personally

like a shot of extra-strong methedrine
so you'll become your own television
Become your own yawn!

O giant yawn, violent revolution
silent television, beautiful poetry
most deadly methedrine
        I choose all of you for my poem personally

## My Kind of Man

I like a man to know a lot more than I do, but I
like him to be pleased and surprised he discovers I
press or sew button in a jiffy.

One thing, I'm bare in bed and he's not thinking
masculine to wash a dish,Ha! Pettiness, Peevishness
and the 'sulks' out! I'd rather have a huge blow-up
planes flying.

If he's talented, that's cute: I put up with a lot.
But he be interested in work, people, life and most of
all me. For I am best. He also have a sense of ridiculous
too. I don't care if he handsome, cozy, sexy or
neat-freak. He just no be vulgar, given to
drink, flirt, drug.

Given this, I hope he surprise me & me feel more
love.

I'm afraid this very minute I won't find this
any man.

*Diaries*

Martha was a girl after my own heart. She slept
late, lived for the moment, and did the thing. Now
this was the truth. We had not known each other long
before we discovered the common bonds. One day was
like this in the diary:

> Got up late. Here I am writing in the
> diary. It is 1:00 PM. It is raining
> outside. Martha is coming over (soon
> I hope). The coffee is boiling so I
> have to go.

Later she showed me her diary:

> Raining outside. Just got up. 1:00 PM.
> Going over to X's soon. Coffee is
> ready.

Then I showed her my diary even later and we agreed
that we had much in common. I asked her about the
X, however, and she said, "You can never tell can
you who might see it?"
    I agreed and since then have been using arbitrary
initials to identify the people in my life.

## Paul Eluard

I have been reading about Paul Eluard tonight.

Did you know he was very large?

Large body, large forehead, large nose.

But not large as a cloud, large as a cloud of smoke.

Large as what, then?

Large as himself.

He was a man irrigated with blood
and turned pink after every meal.

Above greying eyebrows, he had a fine space of forehead
right on up to his hair which is brushed straight back.

(Neither too long, nor too short.)

He wore hats.

He smoked enormously.

He suffered with those who suffer.

(Poets who have suffered are
Lorca, Saint-Pol Roux, Max Jacob, Paul Desnos.)

He did not move without his universe.

He had no money, no papers, no address but
walls covered with Picasso, Miró, Max Ernst, Léger
and original editions which he caressed with his fingertips.

He lived on love, cold water, and poetry.

## * Baby Breakdown *

### for Bill Berkson


lumbering        logging              lonesome

            lugging

                              muggy  weather

numbs my brain

                ha! (a little shout off the machine
                    —thanks   Van)

        separate  sounds  clapping

                        (clap     clap     clap    clap  clap      clap

            inside your head

                            voice line
                            bass line
                            treble line
                            air line

                                            taking off!

you are your head
you are a head
& you are those sounds emanating within

                        SO

                    * GO ON LIVING *

            (more! more! more! more!)

heh!     that guitar just jumped from one ear to the other

& THE GREAT ATLANTIC CABLE IS FREAKING OUT

please don't use that word "freaking" not again
                    Okay

                    The Great Atlantic Cable is nodding out

tho it's not the same thing at all

        PU   AT   IN   ON      YO   EMS

(trans: Put that in one of your poems)

                    Anne,          I think he said

                    & so I did
                    & so it is
                    & so what!

                            so  what?

did you say so what?

                    good morning baby
                    baby  goodnight

good morning baby
baby good night

good night baby
baby good baby

good morning morning
baby good morning

good baby baby
baby good good

good night good morning
good night good night

good baby good
good baby baby

night baby morning
night baby night

18

night night night
morning baby morning

baby baby baby
baby baby baby

morning morning night
night baby morning

baby night baby
morning morning morning

goodbye baby
baby bye bye

good baby morning
good baby night

        baby table
        baby chair
        baby wall
        baby bed

    we're gonna stay here forever so don't wait up

don't get claustrophobic either

    there's a lot of space if you look in the right places

*  (between the lines)  *

        looked & looked

o rapture & destr

    o phantom brain wha     ?

& then something took hold of me  .

       no, not a baby arm

I think it was the BIG REALITY

    (disguised as a baby)

  Lord Lord Lord

I'm so tired
            Now I'm not

                    now I am

    can't decide
                disaster button
                dilemma cushion

    here,

            have a seat in the Magic Tree

    It'll give you a whole new "take" on the situation

                                if you're ready

    I'm sitting here in a completely new place myself tonight

            closer to nature
                    the good-natured "close"

    with a heavy thought on my brain

                it weighs 20 lbs at least

    & has no place to go except the top

            So

            if you see me tomorrow help me out from under

    into the air of your kind gaze

            (Bill)

    warmth surrounds the circle as you cheer them on, em on

                        *

## Pictures From Tofukuji

*for Philip Whalen*

The Buddha is dying

         & all the people are crying

    as well as all the animals

           I see elephant, leopard

jaguar, dove, turkey, monkey, camel, fox, squirrel

    to name a few...

as well as the clouds & trees & breeze — all this "world" creation

      shaking with sorrow

   immutable sun in the sky      just as it should be

    shine on

but what about the hand who draws these quaking lines?

    disappearing behind the clouds

    behind the celebration of

     Buddha's Paranirvana
     completely behind it?

       *

The smaller picture shows metaphysical Buddha

    & the two great bodhisattbas — Manjusri with lion
    & Avalokitesvara with elephant

& lots of other guys who know that they're doing there
    all sitting & standing on some amazing series of cliffs

    ascending clear into your daily consciousness

                              *

We know what we're doing too
carrying firewood from the barn
taking a walk in the bountiful snow
or simply going out to fetch the mail from the large metal
box by the road:
                    811 Fireplace Road

These pictures come all the way from Kyoto, Japan

        where resides the man who sent me them

## Leonardo

winter nights

        old age slumber

                paints embers on the hearth

    a fragile veil of ashes

        the thought of human wings reawakening in him

"Naught do I know

        that which I have known I have forgot

    What right have I to wings?

        the devil take it! the devil take it!
          & free my captive bird"

## Revolution

Spooky summer on the horizon I'm gazing at
from my window into the streets
That's where it's going to be where everyone is
walking around, looking around out in the open
suspecting each other's heart to open fire
all over the streets
                            like streets you read about every day
who are the network we travel through on the way to the center
which is energy filling life
and bursting with joy all over the screen
                                        I can't sit still any longer!

I want to go where I'm not feeling so bad
Get off this little island before the bridges break
(my heart is a sore thing too)
No I want to sit in the middle watching movies
then go to bed in my head
Someone is banging on it with a heavy stick like the enemy
who is he going to be turns into a face you can't recognize
then vanishes behind a window behind a gun
Like the lonely hero stalking the main street
cries out Where are you? I just want to know
all the angles of death possible under the American sky!

I can hardly see for all the buildings polluting the sky
until it changes into a barrage of bottles
then clears up for a second while you breathe
and you realize you're still as alive as ever and want to be
but would like to be somewhere else perhaps Africa
Start all over again as the race gets darker and darker
and the world goes on the way I always thought it would
For the winner is someone we recognize out of our collective past
which is turning over again in the grave

                            It is so important when one dies you replace her
                            and never waste a minute

# GIANT NIGHT

*"There is a river where my soul,*
*hungry as a horse drinks beside me"*

## Going In

We are going in the water for the rest of the day
so that sun so hot now is really a false start
when I mention it on those postcards a week from today
wanting to lighten your feet as you move from town to museum
and taking in a swim you end up in a city which becomes the map
you buy as the water rips at the folds you bend the wrong way
impatient to know the way I stay up studying myself in Europe:

Look at the water splashing from the edge like that!

I can't keep my eyes off summer clothing
or looking for Negroes, say, in Switzerland wondering
what everybody's thinking back in New York a revolution
in my head I'm dreaming everyone is black and here we are
eating a *presso fisso* and dizzy behind the Uffizi
It's all so exhausting with this wine in my feet
and you're dragging me through these Italian streets of sexual freaks
can't believe the skirts I'm wearing and everyone praying
somewhere every day I want to go into the churches they won't let me
like you won't let me bite my nails what fun is that?

But how beautiful everything is and new hitting my eyes
so you can't see yourself getting up at 6:00 AM in Venice
but you do thinking of Stokely Carmichael in London and the part
when he was talking about "history" you know?  and that's what
      we're doing
like tyrants I want it all to be perfect and it isn't
so bad being here, alive and wet all over and you along.

## Paris Day

I've had it here craving for New York City every day
Moving toward atmosphere like the pressure to go out stay in etc.
Yes there are more new movies, people, streets and places
And every morning a newspaper in your native tongue and pills too
But who is dead today that we really care for?
Not George Lincoln Rockwell that horrible creep what else?

Today we went to Sainte-Chapelle, Notre Dame and afterwards
Bought Ted Berrigan a beret and ate those terrific hotdogs
With melted cheese outside the Department Store Hôtel de Ville
By this time it's twelve noon and we're back in the room

Later you're writing poems and I'm reading *Bid Me to Live* by H.D.
Sitting in the Luxembourg Gardens and attacked by these great
        black Algerians
*Vous-êtes Américaine ha ha? Oui, je suis mariée, au revoir.*

Now I'm writing poems and you're reading Boswell's *London Journal*
Unless you're restless and taking a walk in the environs
Let's contemplate postcards to Tom Clark whom we'll see in a week
Or let's miss the radio and Gem Spa and speaking of them
Let's go back immediately!

## Mother Country

What is around me is
this huge shape I can't visualize
from here, sitting here quietly
nights go by the same way
noisy people outside on the block
I want to move from
so I can understand it better

Not all streets are like this one
bursting with so much energy
you can't keep still
with cops watching over every second
nothing gets out of hand out there
but does deep inside you somewhere
down in your American soul

It's hard to kill, harder still to love
where you come from when it hurts you
but you know you do, you do

## Snow

Snow comes down on New York City
the way I imagine the head touches the heart
bending over so gently you hardly notice
your whole body changes clothing
then moves on decisively, a temperature shift
so that you know now how you go
and what you feel is together in itself
a kind of batter pouring into the universe
you will later eat before it is cooked.

## * Giant Night *

Awake in a giant night
is where I am
        There is a river where my soul,
hungry as a horse drinks beside me

An hour of immense possibility flies by
and I do nothing but sit in the present
which keeps changing moment to moment

How can I tell you my mind is a blanket?

It is an amazing story you won't believe
and a beautiful land
where something is always doing in the barns
especially in autumn
        Sliding down the hayrick!

By March the sun is lingering and the land turns wet

Brooks grow loud
The eddies fill with green scum
Crocuses lift their heads to say hello

Soon it is good to be planting
By then the woods are overflowing
with dogwood, redbud, hickory, red and white oaks,
hazelnut bushes, violets, jacks-in-the-pulpit,
skunk cabbages, pawpaws and May apples
whose names thrill you because you can name them!

There are quail and rabbits too — but I go on too long

Like the animal, I must stop by the water's edge
to have a drink and think things over

                    *

That was good. The drink I mean
I feel refreshed and ready for anything

Though I'm not in Vermont or Kentucky unfortunately
but in New York City, the toughest place in the world

And it's December

Here someone is always weeping, including me
though I tend to cry in monster waves then turn into a fish
wallowing in my own salty
                    Puddle! Look out
If you aren't wearing boots you'll be sorry
and soggy too


                        *


This season's cruelty hurts me
and others, I'm sure, who'd rather be elsewhere but can't
because of their jobs, families, friends, money
It's rough anyway you look at it

But what can you do?

It's worse elsewhere, I'm sure

Take Vietnam

No thanks

I think about Vietnam a lot, however
and wonder if I'll ever "see" it
The way I've seen Europe, I mean

Those pretty Dutch girls!
They all ride bicycles

In Venice you travel by boat or foot

The metro and the underground register like the names
in connection with them:

Hugo, Stephen, Stuart, Larry, Lee, Harry, David, Maxine

What does it all mean?

I never ask that, being shy

In this apartment in which I dwell these thoughts pass by

I hope you won't mind the mess when you do too

*

You just walk in up a flight and you're in paradise

A cup of coffee, an easy chair, a loving person waiting for you
who's washing the dishes, reading a book

Outside someone's worrying about love and not sitting down either

He's probably freezing his ass off right now!
And other vital parts which would feel great in the country,
taking a walk, a hike, shoveling snow

Though you can do that right here

*

The hub of the universe is where I am in a night whose promise
grows with me, unlike the snow melting in the gutter

Whatever I do, it is beside me

I look out the window, there is night
I sit in this lighted room knowing this night
Night! Night! I wish you'd go so I could go
to the post office, the bank, the supermarket

Why aren't they open at night? I wonder
Then realize I'm not the only person who's
considered in the grand scope of daily living

There are those fast asleep who want to be and would be horrified
if the post office, the bank, and the supermarket
were only open at night
for you can't be all there all the time

32

I myself am only here part of the time
which is enough
         For there are other places to run to


Uptown, for example, where energy rushes you
like some hideous but intriguing chemical
you can't ignore
and you want to absorb the wisdom these buildings have

How do they feel so high up like that?

Pretty good, they seem to say in their absolute way
But it's the people inside who turn us on

By then you are gone off in a cab
and you are not alone

         I am beside you

The streets are familiar from just traveling through
We rarely stop and when we do there's a reason

Which is too bad
We miss a lot for this same reason

         *


They're probably feeding the chickens about this time
The smell of chicken feed overwhelms me
The rooster crows on a 7th Street fire escape
Breakfast is ready
         There is a forest by the river near the barn
where things are happening,
a whole new world on the edge of dawn

         *

My little world goes on St. Mark's Place

To be not tired, but elated, I sing this song

I think of The Beatles and The Beach Boys
and the songs they sing

It is a different thing to be behind the sound
then leave it forever
and it goes on without them, needing only you and me

Here I am, though you are asleep

The morning of December 3rd dawns on me
in the shape of a poem called "Giant Night"

It must end before it is too late

All over the world children will celebrate Christmas
And families will gather together to give and take this season

Other religions and customs will prevail in their own separate ways
having nothing to do with Christmas

Soldiers will cease fire

Some won't know the difference but might be able to sense it
    in the air

The smell of holly, pine, eggnog
The friendly faces of Santa and his elves

All these will add up to something and be gone forever

Just like what is here one minute and not the next.

# FAST SPEAKING WOMAN

*"I know how to work the machines!"*

## Fast Speaking Woman

"I is another" — RIMBAUD

because I don't have spit
because I don't have rubbish
because I don't have dust
because I don't have that which is in air
because I am air
let me try you with my magic power:

        I'm a shouting woman

        I'm a speech woman

        I'm an atmosphere woman

        I'm an airtight woman

        I'm a flesh woman

        I'm a flexible woman

        I'm a high heeled woman

        I'm a high style woman

        I'm an automobile woman

        I'm a mobile woman

        I'm an elastic woman

        I'm a necklace woman

        I'm a silk scarf woman

        I'm a know nothing woman

        I'm a know it all woman

        I'm a day woman

        I'm a doll woman

        I'm a sun woman

I'm a late afternoon woman

I'm a clock woman

I'm a wind woman

I'm a white woman

I'M A SILVER LIGHT WOMAN

I'M AN AMBER LIGHT WOMAN

I'M AN EMERALD LIGHT WOMAN


I'm an abalone woman

I'm the abandoned woman

I'm the woman abashed, the gibberish woman

the aborigine woman, the woman absconding

the Nubian woman

the antediluvian woman

the absent woman

the transparent woman

the absinthe woman

the woman absorbed, the woman under tyranny

the contemporary woman, the mocking woman

the artist dreaming inside her house


I'm the gadget woman

I'm the druid woman

I'm the Ibo woman

I'm the Yoruba woman

I'm the vibrato woman

I'm the rippling woman

I'm the gutted woman

I'm the woman with wounds

I'm the woman with shins

I'm the bruised woman

I'm the eroding woman

I'm the suspended woman

I'm the woman alluring

I'm the architect woman

I'm the trout woman

I'm the tungsten woman

I'm the woman with the keys

I'm the woman with the glue

I'm a fast speaking woman

                     water that cleans

                     flowers that clean

                     water that cleans as I go

I'm a twilight woman

I'm a trumpet woman

I'm the raffia woman

I'm a volatile woman

I'm the prodding woman

I'm the vagabond woman

I'm the defiant woman

I'm the demented woman

I'm the demimonde woman

I'm the woman deracinated, the woman destroyed

the detonating woman, the demon woman

I'm the lady of the acacias
I'm the lady with the rugs
I'm the accomplished woman
I'm the woman who drives
I'm the alabaster woman
I'm the egregious woman
I'm the embryo woman

I'm the girl under an old-fashioned duress

I'm a thought woman
I'm a creator woman
I'm a waiting woman
I'm a ready woman
I'm an atmosphere woman
I'm the morning star woman
I'm the heaven woman

     that's how it looks when you go to heaven
     they say it's like softness there
     they say it's like day
     they say it's like dew

I'm a lush woman

I'm a solo woman
I'm a sapphire woman

I'm a stay at home woman

I'm a butterfly woman

I'm a traveling woman

I'm a hitchhike woman

I'm a hitching post woman

I'm a sun woman

I'm the coyote woman

I won't be home

I'll be back


I'm a justice woman

it's not sadness

no, it's not a lie


I'm the Southern Cross woman

I'm a moon woman

I'm a day woman

I'm a doll woman

I'm a dew woman

I'm a lone star woman

I'm a loose ends woman

I'm a pale coast woman

I'm a mainstay woman


I'm a rock woman

I'm a horse woman

I'm a monkey woman

I'm a chipmunk woman

I'm a mountain woman

I'm a blue mountain woman
I'm a marsh woman
I'm a jungle woman
I'm a tundra woman
I'm the lady in the lake
I'm the lady in the sand

    water that cleans
    flowers that clean
    water that cleans as I go

I'm a bird woman
I'm a book woman
I'm a devilish clown woman
I'm a holy clown woman
I'm a whirling dervish woman
I'm a whirling foam woman
I'm a playful light woman
I'm a tidal pool woman
I'm a fast speaking woman

I'm a witch woman
I'm a beggar woman
I'm a shade woman
I'm a shadow woman
I'm a leaf woman
I'm a leaping woman
I'M A GREEN PLANT WOMAN

I'M A GREEN ROCK WOMAN
I'm a rest stop woman

I'm a city woman

I long for the country

I get on the airplanes and fly away
I know how to work the machines!
I'm a sighing woman
I'm a singing woman
I'm a sleeping woman
I'm a muscle woman
I'm a music woman
I'm a mystic woman
I'm a cactus woman
it's not strange
no, it's not a lie

I'm the diaphanous woman
I'm the diamond light woman
I'm the adamant woman
I'm the headstrong woman
I'm the tunnel woman
I'm the terrible woman
I'm the tree woman
I'm the trembling woman
I'm the treacherous woman
I'm the touchy woman

            flowers that clean
            water that cleans
            flowers that clean as I go

    I'm an impatient woman
    I've got the right of way
    I'm the baby woman, I'll cry
    I'm the wireless woman
    I'm the nervous woman
    I'm the wired woman
    I'm the imperious woman
    I'm the purple sky woman

    I'M THE PURPLE LIGHT WOMAN
    I'M THE SPECKLED LIGHT WOMAN
    I'M THE SUGAR LIGHT WOMAN
    I'm the breathless woman
    I'm the hurried woman
    I'm the girl with the unquenchable thirst

            flowers that clean as I go
            water that cleans
            flowers that clean as I go

    hey you there
    hey you there, boss
    I'm talking

    I'm a jive ass woman

I'm the callous woman

I'm the callow woman

I'm the clustered woman

I'm the dulcimer woman

I'm the dainty woman

I'm the murderous woman

I'm the discerning woman

I'm the dissonant woman

I'm the anarchist woman

I'm the Bantu woman

I'm the Buddha woman

I'm the baritone woman

I'm the Bedouin woman


I'm the woman with taste

I'm the woman with coral


I'm the mushroom woman

I'm the phantom woman

I'm the moaning woman

I'm the river woman

I'm the singing river woman

I'm the clear water woman

I'm the cleansing woman

I'm the clay woman

I'm the glazed woman

I'm the glass eyed woman

I'm the stone woman
I'm the stone tooth woman
I'm the woman with bones
I'm the fossil woman
I'm the soft flesh woman
I'm the doe eyed woman

      that's how it looks when you go to heaven
      they say it's like softness there
      they say it's like land
      they say it's like day
      they say it's like dew

I'm the lonesome woman
the woman without a home
I'm the lithesome woman
the limber woman, the woman forbidden
the woman divided, the woman entangled
the woman caught between two continents
the woman dancing inside her house

I'm the contented woman
I'm the unrelenting woman
the unresolved woman
the woman with the treble
the soprano woman
the woman who roves
the woman riding in clover

the woman deliberating
the foraging woman
the phenomena woman
the woman who studies
the woman who names
the woman who writes
I'm the cataloguing woman

        water that cleans
        waters that run
        flowers that clean as I go

I'm the vendetta woman
I'm the inventive woman
I'm the invective woman
I'm the reflective woman
I'm the grave miscreant
I'm the molten matter
I'm the substratum
I'm the tumbleweed woman
I'm the half-breed
I'm the banyan tree woman
I'm the static woman
I'm the woman in classic pose

I'm the silk woman
I'm the cloth woman

I'M THE SILVER CLOTH WOMAN
I'M THE GOLD CLOTH WOMAN
I'M THE EMERALD CLOTH WOMAN

I'm the weaving woman
I'm the woman with colorful thread
I'm the fiber woman
I'm the fleeing woman
the woman forgotten
the woman derailed
the tempestuous woman

I'm the woman who dreams
I'm the woman who exhales
I'm the night woman
I'm the black night woman
I'm the night without a moon
I'm the angel woman
I'm the white devil woman
I'm the green skin woman
I'm the green goddess woman
I'm the woman with arms
I'm the woman with wings
I'm the woman with sprouts
I'm the woman with leaves
I'm the branch woman
I'm the masked woman
I'm the deep trance woman

47

I'm the meat woman
I'm the red meat woman
I'm the fish woman
I'm the blue fish woman
I'm the woman with scales
I'm the woman with fins
I'm the crawling woman
I'm the swimming woman
I'm the sunfish woman
I'm the silver fish woman

water that cleans
flowers that clean as I go

I'm the moss woman
I'm the velvet moss woman
I'm the woman with vines
I'm the woman with thorns
I'm the needle woman
I'm the pine needle woman
I'm the science woman
I'm the mistaken woman
I'm the inexorable woman
I'm the explorer woman

that's how it looks when you go to heaven
they say it's like softness there
they say it's like land

they say it's like day
they say it's like dew

I'm the impoverished woman
I'm the heavy belly woman
I'm the woman with hair
I'm the woman with child
I'm the heathen woman
I'm the hermaphrodite woman
I'm the iridescent woman
I'm the hazardous woman
I'm the precipice woman
I'm the insouciant woman
I'm the jasmine woman
I'm the jaguar woman
I'm the Inca woman
I'm the woman with the facade
I'm the woman with the sparks

I'm the taxi woman
I'm the tactile woman
I'm the ductile woman
I'm the taciturn woman
I'm the fierce woman
I'm the Jupiter woman
I'm the tiger woman
I'm the woman with claws
I'm the woman with fangs

I'm the closed circuit woman
I'm the muddy bank woman
I'm the big footed woman
I'm the big hearted woman
I'm the water pool woman
I'm the shimmering woman

I'm flowers radiating light

I'm the heavy paint woman
I'm the patina woman
I'm the matinee woman
I'm the Neanderthal woman
I'm the automaton woman
I'm the decadent woman
I'm the opulent woman

      water that cleans
      flowers that clean
      water that cleans as I go

I'm the beads woman
I'm the stone beads woman
I'm the money belt woman
I'm the woman with the passport
I'm the immigrant woman

I'm the woman with the weight on her shoulders
I'm the woman with the weight on her back

I'm the old woman
I'm the stooped over woman
I'm the barefoot woman
I'm the dark eyed woman
I'm the raven dark woman
I'm the jet black woman

I'm the slippery eel woman
I'm the facile woman
I'm the princess woman
I'm the serpent woman
I'm the ecliptic woman
I'm the sine wave woman
I'm the sliding woman

            waters that clean

            flower that cleans

            waters that clean as I go

I'm the sensible woman
I'm the senseless woman
I'm the pink dawn woman
I'm the mist dawn woman
I'm the mysterious woman
the woman demystified
the woman divulged
the apocalypse woman
I'm the plexiglass woman
I'm the rash woman

I'm the hushed woman

I'm the caustic woman

I'm the resonating woman

I'm the altercating woman

the ambidextrous woman

the ambiguous woman

I'm the effusive woman

I'm the ancipital woman

I'm the woman in the mirror

I'm the woman in the museum

I'm a fast speaking woman


I'm the ameliorating woman

I'm the Marabout woman

I'm the indolent sylph

I'm the frugal handmaiden

I'm the harridan

I'm the trickster

I'm the minx

I'm the shy courtesan

I'm the hausfrau

I'm the woman with the wares

I'm the woman with the whims

I'm the woman with the hems

I'm the woman with the volts

I'M THE POET DREAMING INSIDE HER HOUSE

I'm the tautological woman

I'm the technological woman

I'm the tally sheet woman

I'm the dallying woman

    water that cleans

    flowers that clean

    waters that clean as I go

I'm the magic woman

I'm the fleeting woman

I'm the floating woman

I'm the flotsam woman

I'm the gypsy woman

I'm the rain woman

I'm the rainy season woman

I'm the lady from Twentynine Palms


I'm the inestimable woman I'll convert yr piastres to gold


I'm the Infanta, I'll get my way


I'm the disdainful woman

I'm the declaiming woman

I'm the thwarted woman

I'm the turgid woman

I'm the Tuscarora woman

I'm the farsighted woman

I'm the wry woman

    I'm the circular woman the woman
    who returns

                        water that flows
                        flowers that clean
                        water that flows as I go
I'm the Parnassian woman
I'm the Parsee woman
I'm the monophobic woman
I'm the perfunctory woman
I'm the percussive woman
I'm the domestic woman
I'm the vigilante woman
I'm the chastising woman
I'm the Shakti
I'm the errant woman
I'm the variegated woman

I'm the woman with the clout
I'm the woman with the refrain
                        flowers that clean as I go
                        water that cleans
                        flowers that clean as I go
I'm the hieractic woman
I'm the hermetic woman
I'm the harvesting woman
I'm the cloistered woman
I'm the prismatic woman
I'm the manic woman
I'm the back seat woman

I'm the crusader woman with teapot, bedroll yellow
plastic water bottle & green turban shouting
INSHALLAH on route to El Ayon — reclaim my
Sahara   INSHALLAH!


I'm the old old Polish woman raking & gathering
leaves in mid-October just outside Chicago


I'm the woman scribbling on paper bag sitting by
Hudson, hat slouched over squint in autumn sun


I'm the pinched face lady in Montreal serving you
up a tasty meal

I'm the woman standing in the shadow

the Navajo in velvet


I'm the visceral woman

I'm the Valkyrie

I'm the vermillion woman

the pivoting woman

the Vesuvian woman

I'm the vexed woman

I'm the woman put a hex on you

I'm the concealing woman

I'm the babbling woman

I'm the baksheesh baksheesh baksheesh woman

I'm the bankrupt woman

I'm the bargaining woman

I'm the barracuda woman

I'm the bellicose woman

I'm the benevolent woman

I'm the petulant woman

I'm the aimless woman

I'm the average woman

I'm the woman adoring

the woman adulterated

I'm the acetate woman

The acetylene woman

> water that cleans
>
> flowers that clean
>
> water that cleans as I run

I'm the lone assassin I'll sit in my cell

I'm the inflamed woman ready to burn

I'm the notorious infidel

I'm the agent provocateur

I'm the infectious woman whose energy catches on

I'm the huckster woman just down the street

I'm the woman with the rings

I'm the woman with histrionics

I'm the vixen

the woman in the hovel

the woman on the dole

I'm the regenerative woman

I'm the woman strapped to the machine

I'm the reptile woman I'll grow back my limbs

I'm the reproachful woman I'll never forget

I'm the plutonium woman make you glow for a
quarter of a million years!

I'm the Hottentot woman

I'm the hotrod woman

I'm the hostile woman

I'm the equinox woman

> that's how it looks when you go to heaven
>
> they say it's like softness there
>
> they say it's balanced there
>
> they say it's like land like day like dew

I'm the monophonic woman

I'm the setaceous woman

I'm the moonlit woman in silence under trees

I'm the touchstone woman


I'm the woman with the vitamins

I'm the woman with the keys

I'm the woman with the delays

I'm the woman with the maize

I'm the woman who breathes in

I'm the woman who exhales


I'm the redundant woman

I'm the incumbent woman

the woman askew, the woman amok

the amorous woman

the malachite woman

the hidden cave woman

THE WOMAN INSPIRED INSIDE HER HOUSE!

I'm the volcano woman

I'm the pressured woman

I'm the bituminous woman

I'm the slimy fuel woman

I'm the bright fire woman

I'm the fire eater woman

I'm the spaced out woman

I'm the hemmed in woman

I'm the woman with the walking shoes

I'm the woman with the straw hat


I'm a fast speaking woman

I'm a fast rolling woman

I'm a rolling speech woman

I'm a rolling water woman


I KNOW HOW TO SHOUT

I KNOW HOW TO SING

I KNOW HOW TO LIE DOWN


Note:

"Fast Speaking Woman" is indebted to the Mazatec Indian shamaness, Maria Sabina, in Mexico guiding persons in magic mushroom ceremony & is a reworking & coincidence of the same for all wandering spirits.

## Battery

A trio of instruments you love the notes
indissectible & extending small rockets of delight
force to love, be loved, love accelerating
love momentum, the love to travel
we will never agree the world contains
so much phenomena we'll put on glasses
abstract it give it structure make a frame
inversely proportional to the square of
two distances apart
make us a family of celestial bodies that we
be one we ellipse about a warming sun
love that sun
dual nature of electrons heal us o heal us
I would come back not hide be in motion
I would attach myself to home again
I would be sister mother lover brother
I would be father I would be infant animal awesome
I would suffer & become extinct again
I would relight the earth with love
I would be still I would be silent & quake
I would be afraid but not for love for
the many manifestations glowing faces
Love the notes as they pour like water
love the water under your feet & when
you look look with eyes of love
all the layers, the ground under
your feet & under the ground
the imagined creatures
& above your feet the grasses the
watercress so fine to eat &
see the roots & bottom of pleasure
of moss look into pleasure the color
disappearing or changing the light
love the light & see the sky the scaffolds the planets
the length the width the distance
the congruity the parallels the fracture
love the body keep it elastic
keep it dancing rallying on its own

keep it safe from harm from red tape
& those next to you be kind be quiet
be exalted be a charm a fusion be a battery
be insistent be an empire be a symphony
& in a moment's gentle passing
& in a moment's violent passing completely
be her be him be them, see the face beneath
the face & see with eyes of love, gaze straight
into eyes of love with eyes of love

## Musical Garden

Can't give you up, can't stop
    clamoring

Can't give you up, sweetheart, my tender
    chocolate big-lipped love

Can't give you up, all dear ones, your bright
    ears & delicate smiles

Can't give you up, Louis-Ferdinand Céline,
    you're obsessed & vitriolic & absolutely
    right

Can't give you up, random motion, lucky choices,
    air rides, dominoes, structural linguistics

Can't give you up yet, rum, the bottle's not
    empty & it's warming me

Can't give you up night mail, telephone ringing,
    talking about Kerouac

Can't give up messiness, compulsion, confusion,
    pressure, misery, indulgence

Can't give you up, memory, & murderous dreams
    in which my being's dismembered

Can't give you up, de-animation love

Can't give up the color blue — never never never

Can't give up Andhra Pradesh, weep for India's
    starving, going blind no vitamin A
    so necessary, weep for Pakistan flood victims,
    homeless, homeless, homeless

Can't give it up, a propensity for travel,
        moving speedily to friends at every turn,
        scenes, situations I'm not even needed

Can't give it up, heritage, ailanthus trees,
        radial symmetry, bamboo

Can't give up fertility—no way

Can't give you up yet, best jewels, assets,
        secret notebooks, masks

Can't give you up, dinosaur obsession, my jaw
        strangely prominent with carnivore teeth

Can't give up outrage or outrageous behavior &
        I'll go dancing & wailing for that!

Can't give you up dreamers, inventors, scientists,
        deceivers, iridescent dolphins
        & especially bottlenose dolphin with
        mouth like my lover's

Can't give you up, black magic fantasies I'll
        make everyone collapse & revive & they'll
        get wiser

Can't give it up, make time stop

Can't do it, ordinary consciousness, I'm trying
        but it's so hard

Can't give you up, musical garden: Bach, Beethoven,
        Buddy Holly, Robert Johnson, Jelly Roll
        Morton!

Can't give up sitting in a hammock in the fifties,
        I was a babe enjoying solitude—
        hummingbirds

Can't give you up, canyon dream, I'm in between
        there are turtles & little prairie mutations

Can't give up chiffon, sable, inarticulateness,
  simple solid reason, logarithms, furry
  California mountains, not brooding but
  simmering, zeroing in, conquest,
  retreat, romance

Can't give it up, the proposal closest to my heart,
  signs saying Detective Agency in L.A., stop-
  lights, Mercedes, folk fiddling from Sweden

Can't give up Orissa state, prostrations
  optical illusions, fan mail, trekking old
  Inca trails, greasy Tibetan tea, schedules
  to win & lose by, the phases of the moon,
  firebrand meteors, the Kentucky Derby,
  gambling, the ruins of Pisac, Peru with stones
  so red & polished & finally honed I ambled
  about all afternoon

Can't give you up Baltic Sea, migrations, go-between,
  well-wishing, living on the edge of Harshness
  Street

Can't give it up,foxy, classy, flashy, bratty

Can't give you up books, bees, Latin derivatives,
  Quechua, stationery, habit, responsibility,
  squabbling, bubbling on till dawn, metal plastic,
  electricity rush, melodrama, poverty, the high
  life, humor, privacy, cynicism, doubt but no
  boredom

Can't give you up, solar energy, speech, and more
  speech & more speech & more energy more
  sunlight more emergency can't give you up
  can't give it up yet won't do it won't do it
  can't give it up yet won't give you up yet
  can't give it up!

## Light & Shadow

Rest you by this various planet
or lounge in the sky lounge
be my guest I'll take you there
& introduce you around & show
you the sky ropes & the
city maps and the world
as round as a lively face
with head & atmosphere
& the sky as breath and the river
as chant and the sun as aria
aria for breathing and for loving
aria for the dancing light & shadow
light & shadow upon the dancing globe
light & shadow on the child's arms
in a park under trees & towers,
light on the fresh canvas, the painter
on the roof of West 21st Street
under thoughtful shadow,
shadow on spoons in the metal drawer
the zebra plant yearning for light
light for the ears of Beethoven, shadow
inside the piano, mellow now violent
shadow out of the piano, power in the
light of the violin, sweet strings of light,
shadow under my desk, big black boots in winter,
light through friendly words
on shadowy telephone wires,
light in health & shadow in health,
illuminate moon rocks! knowledge from shadow,
light from darkest handwriting, print as light
and white paper, shadow
light from newly polished floors, shadow
in your smile under heavy lids,
cadenza light, shadow on the line of scrimmage
melodious indestructible Vajra songs!
slabs of colored light on the horizon,
the shadow of the big plane on the ground below
a single light in the mosque, shadow in the carved lace

on Persian screens, geometric light on tiles,
light through stained glass windows, light streaming
through reels of shadowy celluloid
lights dimming in overworked cities,
shadows in villages, no light but one
butter lamps, the black hole of Calcutta
birds in flight, the elephant's slow-moving shadow
the imprint of Sappho, bird scratches
Haydn's *Mass in Time of War*
Leewenhoek's back bending to study microscopic shadows,
lights from headlights, gels for colored light
silver light, winter day, the sun's in Scorpio
golden light, Colorado desert, the sun's incessant
volcano Cotopaxi gleaming, active shadow
through the molten cone
Venus big as searchlight August 1974, dawn,
& bright as the crescent moon!
dim rings of Saturn, Mars reddish light twinkling
in the dense night
light refracted through cloudy shattered glass,
phosphorus glittering in the Mediterranean
the mineral lightning bug glowing on the farmhouse floor
the owl's slow hoot from the forest shadows,
inexplicable X-rays, shadows on the lung
doubt, despair, danger, beware shadows before a storm
shadow of wide-awake country fly on ceiling 3:00 AM
chemistry, campfires, insanity, flashlights
Christopher Smart on his knees in mad poetic fervor
Virgil, the unmasked hero
Emma Goldman an open book
more names: Gertrude Stein, Mozart, Wittgenstein, Whitman
Cecil Taylor's white jazz light, wave-breaking fingers
on the black & white keys
white egrets nesting on redwoods, a loud flutter
of big wings, of shadow on the green as they head out
toward the lagoon
ultraviolet light radiating from lupine, shadow of
the insects attracted, preparing to land
blue lights at the airport
shadow I'm wearing of our parting

shadow I'm wearing of our parting
glories in the sky raining down all silver & golden
shadows between fingers, between breasts, between legs
shadows of monoliths, the monuments
the Leaning Tower of Pisa, the Eiffel Tower
the Camera Obscura in Edinburgh
quaint shadows of mushrooms, tops of amanita
shining like silver moon in moonlight,
bright red by day!
Dr. Anton Mesmer experimenting in the chill wind . . .
Apollinaire drunk, Mayakovsky talking to the sun
Rimbaud, bright youth visionary
Pound's silent presence
Willliam Carlos Williams's "Atta boy! Atta boy!"
St. Teresa, a candle, shadow on the mast
death by drowning, a charmed life
shrouded, umbrella'd, sheltered
light from the Himalayas, the Andes
the brightness of snow, the shadows cast by
mountains, by fast moving clouds, the shadow
of stormy Arabs, surefooted Balinese,
Cicero's light now fading, Galileo's vision,
the long shadow of Jesus, Locke's reasoning
light, Homer's voyaging light & shadow
Aristotle, dark & consuming
the shadow of Freud turning the century
Goethe's elective affinities
Newton's arrogant light
Calvin's stoic light & stiff shadow
poor Abelard suffering under prison's damp shadow
Socrates' wise forehead, Einstein's brain the speed
of light, Aquinas, Plato, Pasteur all
lightbulbs in the brown study, a dark laboratory
Herodotus collecting light: knowledge of
cats, Egypt's black ways & foreign women,
Dante spiraling upward to stars,
Darwin, Rousseau, Descartes all thinking
in their armchairs,
Michelangelo lifting his brush to
paint a body's shadows, Leonardo inventing
contemplating wings of light

66

Milarepa composing on the snowy mountain,
names names once men & women who walked in daily light & shadow
with light for the modern world,
without gravity, light enough to float
without sun, no shadow
sun on all the wonders of the world
the pyramids casting their shadow in the morning
the buildings blocking my shadow with their shadow
the light of sound, a KLH, a radio box, magnetic tape
the shadowy TV, sinister propaganda parading as light
a devastated land the sun still shines
bloodshed on the land, shadow
on the American soul, the diamond spirit
of warriors glinting in the sun under evil glare,
shadows in houses when it's always raining,
light reflecting off pools of rain, shadows
of passing traffic of big fur coats, slender
shadows at the beach, a flame in a room
without electricity, shadow on the page of
Stendhal I'm reading, shadow of your head
against a stucco wall, light in the dreams
of martyrs, shadows from their fiery death
at the cruel stake, light on the crystal on
the brain! shadow at the back of the mind
trying to remember something,
shadow in the mouth, a doctor's light
on the polished teeth, in a troubled ear,
black holes, white holes, silver bullets
light on the edge of night
the shadow of the moon,
an eclipse for the total world
shadows in notebooks in matchbooks
till you open them, in the heart until it opens
to light the eyes of the person you love,
the tall shadow of people of trees of rockets
of obsolescence of plastic of neon of laser beams
of solar flares
the light that turns you around
that shock that blinds
that draws your hands up to your eyes

& you run for shadow
the light of women radiating with all
their wholeness, with soft ground-control
light, men's light of clarity, penetration,
a shiny helmet, fucking on the edge of
night, night on the edge of shadow,
the innate shadow of cities, the hidden light
of cities, the shadow in the valley,
the shadow the horse makes running
the swift hunter's eyes darting between
light & shadow, the shadow the gull
makes, the crow, the eagle, the vulture
the light glistening on the wet seals
playing on the San Francisco coast,
the shadows furniture makes
in all the living rooms all across the world,,
the shadows huts make, the light absorbed
into clothes, the women in South America
beating their clothes against the rocks
drying them in sun & sitting down in shadow,
the cool shadows of water, fish illuminated,
their colors brilliant in the glittering light
through the clear sea, darting in & out of
light & shadow, shadow from the tender water plants
swaying in the tender light & shadow

# SUN THE BLOND OUT

for Douglas Dunn

*Followe thy faire sunne, unhappy shadowe*

— THOMAS CAMPION

## Slowly,

the first page only for you
the astonished eye it's all you
sunny taste you & touch this memory down
suppose a collapse deceived into thinking
you have progressed in rubbed purr
a special antelope you are
It is June as I write
I sit inside the blond before you
after you, beside you
your light is sharp & gentle
in crystal tales in cool palatial light
it's all love shimmering, clouds racing
over  mountains  someplace     here     now
For them.       For you.
more in any wetness, summer begins
or long ago.

## Sun the Blond Out

That's my mind out nines in coke
blue boxes of Ralph Waldo, the PEOPLE people
A year ago I smelled the wild columbine
& the Lutherans have built "Anne! Anne!"
a lively-haired lady to leave these strokes out
circa sipping iced tea by the blond
Tough leather trees down
Canyon to Austin, Kertesz photo around the turn or
postcard of bearlike person with someone else in car
The buffaloes are not what yes or title, yes
My sweet one laid up in Secua, Ecuador
I like this one Five Spot write religion out while
a man slipped white crosses to the Responsible One
coming for interview Remember Some Apartments 10:45 AM
Bright African dancing mountains & today 2 rains
In the Baths last night not to get violent
anarchy touches wire or scare up a storm
"sun the blond out sun the blond out"
halter strands suds the Publisher-Pusher
Blue hero passes, youthful Italian Infanta says
"The President's not in here, thank you, Mister"
A woman waits or bird over bridge
as I exit he drives upon the buffalo
making a good cover America's thinking but
wooden hearts I saw in Sun Ra's jungle dark hair
rich pieces of orchestra shimmer in this century only.

## & do what I know best

actually, and weeping do nothing best
but love you best
the birds like flutes winding down
& see these things for you
your face the wind makes
more light rain
*la dolce rima d'amore*
how careful I was but now
against that time
I write these things for you
your leg around my river body
walk thru the night, move your legs
I move my legs
& the stars at solstice
you laugh

             *

     such a jolt
my love of dance
perhaps another dance
your hands walk in patience

holding Edwin's hand
my love
where have you been
nothing I've seen
in Boulder
no end to

walking, such a jolt
perhaps the dance
where you've been
no end to
holding Edwin

## Distance Traveled

Hoist sail, little bark of my wit!
Little Captain gazing 'round—
How can I speed without you?
The light of the moon rising in Aries
makes me set a face to the hillside
Nor was our parting over
at the foot of the mountain.

## For J.A. As Dusk Deepens Canyon

This time we were passing into night
climbing down    many gestures in blue
his eyes & scary shadows
the weed we smoked?        egg of a moon?

(One of the guards rubbed crushed leaves of a shrub
on our scratches & cuts
without any show of feeling or favor)

Will the Ashbery group please assemble
to hug the road & sing to flowers
obscure at dusk?

Yellow  monkeyflower

Western golden ragwort

Scarlet gilia

Rocky Mountain bee plant

Pyrola

## Throw matches at the sun!


& vanish to Casper, the Grasslands, Otsego County
    the voice demands dinner
       & how shall I survive?
I unfold this in plunges
in the company of flesh & willful concertos
    gold hair'd angel infancy demanding
      summer's honey breath


        *


these people storm into my life
& beat the wind with blows

    Salt Lake City is transported
further from my sight to Truckee
where it's taking him

Love alters not wetness
in words
eyes flashing
    she drives upon the buffalo


        *


caressed you curiously, gush history
but lie here with the gold
wild Indian don't move like stallions
or did, my heart not shoulder high
this heart moves its head from side to side
opens doors or sets a clock
authority dream figures, hallucinations
your transparent skin, Pale Traveler.
Dear D: this may be said to be ready
and if resisting, have no thought
but face a roof of notes above the world.

# JOURNALS & DREAMS

*"& I smelled the killer petrochemicals and I wasn't assured"*

## George Sand

disguised bravado     all doors open     revise or polish
incandescent spirit     too impatient     profanity's released
            my genius
no genteel poverty (a woman's)     or plan     no seamstress
or mechanic     walking the Boulevards     virility absorbed
    visiting libraries     imprecise clever words
decorating snuff boxes     I enjoy with impunity
            lovers     lacking artifice
    the aura of a man     self-reliant     enterprising
unabashedly romantic *Indiana*     fame overnight activates
    the steel button, my mind     my mistress's blue-black hair
(Marie Duval)     souvenir of clinging mist     Sainte-Beuve
Jules     Prosper Merimée     iconoclasts     roués     rakes
self-irony not exempt     Alfred de Musset     I sigh
"Just another importunate bore"     delirium     to tantalize posterity
hysteria     15 pages a day or die     I write
            Marie Comtesse d'Agoult
    pale imitation     abstruse decline     revengeful daughter
frail Chopin     survival of me     the toughest
            sexless eroticism

## Divorce Work

This is an energy crisis

*Se habla español*

*Aviso a Todos Clientes:*

NO TIRE LA PUERTA

POR FAVOR VENGA A ESTA VENTANILLA

I'm the whitest lady in the room, the whitest lady
getting a divorce the whitest lady at the little window
When you can't afford a lawyer come here come get it here
When you don't have hundreds of dollars get it on over here
on East 2nd Street, the end of Western Civilization, New York

In this bitter light I banged my body around ripped the phone
again & smashed a chair    everything got red      the avaricious
& the prodigal          against a better will the will fights ill
against a better will ill mights will    against my pleasure
I moved on as one goes by a wall close to the battlements
people distilled thru my eyes, drop by drop, the evil fills
the whole world, drop by drop I went on and heard the shades
weeping & complaining:

   "this is what you get for being so kind"
   "if Puerto Rico isn't free in five years I'll be dead"
   "if the President had the power of King Henry, they'd
   surely have no heads!"
   "I'm a Madras coolie, I'm a Madras coolie
   I'm hungry, I'm hungry"
                     &  so  on

I looked into their eyes. Was I the root of this evil tree?
I called on all deities wrathful & compassionate and none came.
Had I walked too far? These words shall not be without reward
if I return to complete the short way of that life flying to
its end. These words shall not be. There was no new senator

I wanted   there was a new governor I didn't care   there was
the beginning of a subway to be completed in 1988 and if I'm
here I'll be crazier & if Puerto Rico isn't free in 5 YEARS I'LL
be dead
               avarice quenching love for every good

And so I turned to the stars to understand division to understand
divorce
          disasters      *des asters*


                    a radical separation
     *divorciar   divertir*
separate   divert
                *no problemes*
desire not to stay longer
                    to stay this contract longer to stay
this agreement
               just so you know it's just recent a lady gets back
her name, her maiden name just recent
                         antiquated   the   lady   said
especially in adultery, abandonment, cruelty, violence
it's usually the lady


    Observe the Milky Way at all times of year
& you will observe variables
plot these variables, their change in brightness
& when a nova has been announced
                         observe it
               & make your own light curve


This is an energy crisis
This is an energy crisis
aerosol cans destroy the ozone
I bring my mortal body thru this world
2 secretaries typing
& another filling out forms in Spanish about cruelty & possessions
I want the house & the car & the TV one lady said
He stopped loving me, I knew it, I said fuck it

I just noticed the ceiling disappears      it goes way up to a rotting
darkness

many chains come down on which the walls are suspended
suspended we're suspended
the partitions within a labyrinth of partitions parting we're
officially parting      it's made legal      it's the end of a 7-year
contract   abandonment   I'm sorry    I love you      went to Europe
went to California     just kids       we sit under fluorescent
on multicolored bubble seats   it's never been a pleasant business
it's a business after all     What a way to split  amicably
And what's a marriage anyway? Get married to commit adultery?
Everyone loves an adulteress so they can talk      Everyone loves
a white adulteress

So it's A for adultery & A for avarice and & A for abandonment
Everyone loves a white adulteress

against a better will the will fights ill
distilling thru my eyes, tears for this whole world

## White Eyes

Friends & Relatives:
Do not try to sort out acknowledging you've traveled to the other
side of the shore do not dissolve
     see your unborn children in their eyes — 3, and then 2
and 1, and then 1 and 1 and 1, and then dissolve
     watch them drive up see their guns, see
unborn children see them dissolve
     poison green sky dissolve
it's a negative sky it's all wrong it's the pits I cut off all reactions
     in my mind . . .
I write it off in my mind . . .
     cruising cops . . .
It's a hard life. I won't dissolve here. Dissolve into her if at all.

        *

Story: I go with the guys to the Falls. I go with my friend Little
Bee. We fix our eyebrows but we don't exercise. We lie around
and compare. We drink & smoke & read a little. We always eat
fuller out. We have a refrigerator but no conditioner. We eat
milk. We share a room but we use the beauty parlor. We work a
lot. It's a hard life I like it. I think I've always lived here. I watch
them come & go and there's always the other girls don't speak
much and Mr. Leon the boss says I'm lookin' good and all my
glitter. We go with the guys & let ourselves be photographed in
front of the Falls when the lights are on (we've crossed over,
we're in Canada now) and when it's white it's scary and when
it's blue it's hidden and when it's pink I'm silly and when it's
white again it's time to go. I have a little picture of myself in
front of a black cloud.

        *

PEOPLE THE INVISIBLE WORLD WITH SPIRITS

I can see the sky this morning
freshness & change

let it sleep and then let it awake again is what I say
for if it could be seen if it could be heard if it could be felt
I could generate
I could generate & then I could rest & you wouldn't be idle
anymore
& I'd have done
I'd have done my best but these are
coincidences
these are the stories of the red races
they lived, they generated and
this was a story about the food: There were three sisters — the Spirit
of Corn, The Spirit of Beans and the Spirit of Squashes. They had
the forms of beautiful females and were very fond of each other and
delighted to dwell together & their apparel was made of the leaves of
their plants and in the growing season they visited the fields because
they were happy there.

This triad was *De-o-ha-ko,* which means Our Life,
Our Supporters and they were never spoken of separately, except
by description as they had no individual names.

*

Virescent water, virescent sky and if you're on the edge you won't
have to plunge in

things are separate do something about it

name it one name    name it one name
name it a name no more presumptuous
than the wind in the leaves

I live on Planet Earth, I have little delicate ears,
let us abide in anger now

So how I got here is I met a man at a party. So how I got here is
I got a letter. I got a letter requesting to be here. I could work.
I would get money. I could bring my friends. I have a grand
trine in fire. It's who I am. I can go almost anywhere.

Travel to the other
            side of the shore not acknowledged.


                            *


The Princess marries the Old Man and there's no choice, bent on
self-destruction.
                    but it's a success story:

A young maiden residing at Ga-u-gwa, a village above Niagara
Falls at the mouth of the Cayuga Creek had been contracted
to an old man of ugly manners & disagreeable person.
Because by the customs of the Nation there was no escape,
she resolved upon self-destruction. Launching a bark canoe into
the Niagara she seated herself within it and composed her
mind for the frightful descent down the current. The rapid
waters soon swept her over the Falls and the canoe was
seen to fall into the abyss below but the maiden had
disappeared. Before she reached the waters underneath she
was caught in a powerful blanket by He-no The Thunderer
and his two assistants and carried without injury to the home of
the Thunderer behind the Falls. Her beauty attracted one of
the dependents of He-no and The Thunderer willingly
adjoined them in marriage.

For several years before this event, the people at Ga-u-gwa had
been troubled with an annual pestilence and the source of the
scourge had baffled all conjecture. He-no revealed to the
maiden the cause and the remedy. He told her that a monstrous
serpent dwelt under the village and made his annual repast
upon the bodies of the dead which were buried by its side. That
in order to ensure a bountiful feast he went forth once a year

83

and poisoned the waters of the Niagara and also of the
Cayuga Creek whereby the pestilence was created. He-no gave
the Princess careful instructions touching the education of the
child of which she was to become the mother. With these
directions she departed on her mission back to her people.

After her nation had removed as directed, the great serpent
disappointed of his food put his head above the ground to
discover the reason and found the village was deserted. Having
scented their trail and discovered its course he went forth into
the lake and up the Buffalo Creek in open search of his prey. It
was in this narrow channel He-no discharged upon the
monster a terrific thunderbolt which inflicted a mortal wound.

*

one view out the window is not enough        one wound is healing

   the gap comes to you, not flashing, it comes to you

      ordinary mind
            panic
                 it accommodates sky it accommodates

clouds and we are known for not keeping secrets we white
conquerors we chalk and dust. So now we are plundering, so now
we are poisoning so now we'll turn it all wrong and we'll
let everybody know how to murder the sky and water

*

So here's how I continued here. I got to the airport and I met
my friend and then we got on a plane and got to the next airport
and met our friend. I was 1 and then we were 2 and now we
are 3 in a strange place. Constellation of 3. We arrived and we
got guided and we got taken and we got put away. Put away and
not a bite to eat. We laughed a lot and we had beer. We had
company and we were company and we went out to see the food
and stars. We walked to two lights we thought were food.

We came back. We took off all our clothes and lay in bed not breathing. A tiny cell, like India. A tiny cell, South America. A tiny cell in St. John's, Canada. A tiny cell for little problem boys. Bunks and a table & a closet & no air. And I saw them in my head and they were standing there, the ghost tanks, the monolithic ghost tanks, obsolete maniacal ghost tanks & I smelled the killer petrochemicals and I wasn't assured. I got sick & I dissolved and I had a blissful dream in which I arrived at a place where you could live without breathing and that was the death body-state & then I awoke.

*

Let me read my work to myself let me explain let me show myself it's all in the way you dream

   and we'll go with the guys to the other side

  Speak, okay: speaking: okay, I'm speaking and if I'm speaking I'm speaking to YOU

      the rising cities of the North
the first lights of the Industrial Revolution

    the rising cities of the North not a way
    to go

not a way to go unconscious I dreamt Four Corners
& there are Four Corners & 4 Disasters & 4 Death Body-States
  to the East, a state of callousness embodying openness

to the West, open secrets
    to the South, curry favor
to the North, harpoons

   Let me go
    & so on

not a way to dream unconscious I dreamt  Vertical Currents

*

conclusions reached by reflective mind
under inspiration of nature

       for example: the colors are all wrong

  no birds
      example: it's a possibility

    example: there's a house & there's a sacred place & there's
a burial mound

      example: there's a sacrifice

So, the memory of what one planned to do & what one plans
   is  indistinguishable

        & the sky reeks & the antennas are
        mystical

& every moment is coming to life & are you listening, now are
you  listening?

    let's go out to prepare the day for a new look at Man

& let's go to the Falls, the big steel Falls

  & let's listen to the rocks & make them skip & hop


       *


So we arrived, we got dressed & this is what we saw

      speed

      debutantes

     the original site

a person making a house & a sacred ritual ground
a person making a miniature house & a miniature sacred ritual
           ground

      & he's one tribe

a person making pools to collect the constellations
& she's another
glass refracting and a packaged destroyed house hit by thunder

these are clues & if you walk you'll rest, you'll stop & see

we are living & moving & collecting & walking & disturbing

Buena Vista room 14 one window collect the information and
make it work

phonecalls to the petrochemicals
& here's the list from the petrochemicals:

photofabrication of small metal parts
photochemical  fabrication
heat exchangers, examporators, driers, pumps
fiberglass reinforced polyester, vinyl ester & epoxy tanks
chemical resistant ducts & tanks
march magnetic chemical pumps
steel & alloy vessels, shell & tube heat exchangers
special process equipment of nickel, monel-iconel-copper
stainless  steel-clad
steel-steels & ASME code welding
pressure vessels, heat exchangers
fabrication & installation of piping systems
corrosion resistance for the chemical industry
ampco metal sewage equipment
fabricators, aluminum, stainless steel
ASME, code welding, steel & all alloys, pressure vessels
chemical resistance coating
dyes for all industries, specialty chemicals
petrochemicals
aromatic, aliphatic solvents, aromatic chemicals, butadiene
isophthalic acid, MEK, olefins, resins, surfactants
ascension  chemicals
petroleum solvents & chemicals
tank wagons, drums & carboys
sodium hypochlorite, caustic soda

swimming pool chemicals, muriatic acid, sulphuric acid,
nitric acid
ammonia
metal treating chemicals
commercial & proprietaries
alcohols, acetates, amines, aromatic & chlorinated solvents, ethers,
glycols, glycol ethers, ketones, naphthas, plasticizers, resins,
terpenes, waxes, thickeners
metal cleaning compounds
cleaners, fertilizers, ammonia
industrial reagent dry & liquid chemicals
industrial & heavy chemicals for every purpose
raw materials
Diamond Shamrock Chemical Co.
coal chemicals
chemicals, solvents, plastics, metals, packaging
adhesives, antifreezes, antiknocks, explosives, fabrics,
coated fabrics, fibers, films (industrial,
packaging, photo), paints, pigments, plastics, propellants
refrigerants, rubbers (synthetic), solvents,
industrial & laboratory chemicals
oxygen & acetylene order department, over 1,000 items available!
chemical surplus salvage residues
pigments, fillers, resins, pails & drums serving paint, rubber,
plastic ink, adhesive, coating industries
metals, coal, oil, gases, foods, salt spray testing (labs)


          a list of romances, suicides and honeymoons
       a list of disturbances
                    powerplants
                              get a telescope
converting sand to glass etc.
                         a list of friends & relatives
Tuscarora
          the Rickards etc.
list of ammunitions
          what's in the black plastic bags of the border patrol?
get their licenses etc.


               sine waves

get the circuits from Max

Charley has been here all summer & knows some history . . .

> I want to stay in the forever situation
>       continuity & change

Courier Express Saturday August 31:
Niagara Falls, Ontario — A body removed from the forebay at the
Sir Adam Beck power generating station in Queenston has been
identified as Grant Chatting, 16, of 8793 Willoughby Drive here.

>   This is not to depress you this is to release you
> & we write to get it over, get on with it

Police believed the youth jumped or fell into Chippewa Creek
and was carried by the swift current into the canal which flows
into the hydroelectric plant.

>       are you listening?        are you panicked yet
> are you facing the void?    spiral currents
>                             vertical drop 350 ft.
>                             are you scared yet?

I am the princess under the Falls I go down I come up 3 sweaters

3 seats for anything you've got

3 in the motel in the Forever Situation


                            *


So we moved. We spent all our money. We paid our way and
made lists. We wrote in notebooks and unconscious we
dreamt resplendent things. Silver water cascading down to a
silent place. Mist maiden, a tree hung around my neck.
Chalky books, the poet howling in the dark, etc. Saxbe wants
National Police Force, Canadian helicopter on its constant
round. Vertiginous. Virescent. A far cry.
Hennepin. Gillette. The purple & white rope in the Afghani

store. Opulence. A funny honeymoon. Hopewellian.
Stella Niagara. Madame Tonti with her perishables

    moving o'er the wistful sky

An age shall come the years gliding away when the automaton
will rise & I said to the operator it's

    B for boy
    O for oil
    L for love
    I for innocence
    N for nation
    A for ancestor
    S for slipping away

       & all the time thinking:
disembodied Kerouac, disembodied Kerouac
    little ballet dancer with the big calf

whirlpools & dizziness & if you're listening
    I'll make my speech

Let me make this over again Let me make it up Let me spin
Let me address you & make you smile & make you wiser
but you'll have to weep first
& go down under the Falls.

              *

FRIENDS & RELATIVES:

We have reason to glory in the achievements of our ancestors.
We put our masks on & we are death connected but it's when the
world was steady. When the world was steady. Now I behold
with sadness the present declining state of our noble race. Once
the warlike yell and the painted band were the terror of the
white man. Then our fathers were strong and their power was felt
and acknowledged far and wide over the American continent.
But we have been reduced and broken by the cunning and

rapacity of the white skinned race. We are not compelled to
crave as a blessing that we may be allowed to live upon our own
lands, to cultivate our own fields, to drink from our own springs
and to mingle our bones with those of our ancestors. Many
winters ago our wise ancestors predicted that a great monster
with white eyes would come from the East and as he advanced
would consume the land. They advised their children when they
became weak, to plant a tree with four roots, branching to
the North, the South, the East and the West and then collecting
under its shade to dwell there in peace and harmony. Here
we will gather here live here die.

*

So we arrived & stayed & wrote these things

We lost the touch for land and we lost the touch for gold & glitter
& we painted our nails as a celebration we painted our nails as
a parody and we were celibate, me and Little Bee

    we crossed the border and didn't get acknowledged

we crossed over & having done we slept and dreamed Thunder

And in the end it was Thunder & in the end it was all Thunder
& in the end it was Thunder & in the end it was undone
undone sky I dreamt unconscious

    & I was humbled before that standing within me
which speaks with me

    I floated up & over into Air
& everybody was watching.

## Mirror Meditation

Look at my face
you have aged me you have aged me

lines of suffering lines where tears
ran & continue streaming
rivers & canals of the woman the woman
who weeps the women who weep
over this whole world crying

                    you did this!

you do this and don't remember
telling me

                    you do it to me
                    do it to yourself

                    you did this!

There's a mirror, silver, I look
to find myself

                    you do this!

and I go into my parallel universe,
silver, and there's water
but there's no talking there

not lonely but alone
and suspended
not studying myself
not staying awake studying myself
just alone, aging

                    you did this!

your mouth and your cunt

you did this!

It's a mercy killing it's
absolute & adamant

   do it!

Take a look at my fragments
you have aged me  you have aged me
take my fragments  do this  take me

 it's a face

a face by nature's own hand
mirrored  crying

   do it!

face me

 do it to me
 it's you
 face me

rivers and canals of the
subtle woman body

streams by nature's own hand
painted

 silver

silver for solitude

silver for ice

I don't like rain but I still like ice

My vices are little girls
and that within you like fire

some small fires
some small fires

That within you I saw and led astray
so it won't come back to me forgive me
forgive myself

you do this!
you did this!
do it!

led astray no memory

so I can't say "I love your memory" anymore

slips away

and the face too, weeping translucent
blood

all the blood sucked away

which explains headaches & the head's
extreme volition to pain

all the blood sucked away

and the dream of the plucked dancing girl
all the hairs plucked away

from she who bristled like a wild animal

from she who danced, once
got sucked away

I watched the pores, as if
through a microscope

bloodless, I dreamt

plucked and sucked away

a little wild animal, wild
from concentration on the dance

it was her whole life

    you did this!
    you do this!

suck yourself away

No talking but sucking sounds
in this other universe

              I'll stay

sucking sounds from the mouths
and pores absorbing the weeping
of the other universe

So when I say "good luck"
I'm talking to myself and
may you have guidance, like starlight,
along the way

So when I say nothing, I'm
nothing to myself and may you
be nothing in the way

No memory


                you did this!

sucking yourself away

The parents give you body
but not your subtle jumping mind

              you do this!

suck yourself away

mercy killing more mercy, killing

        you do this!

suck me away

and the body moves towards decay
and the mind's still dancing
and the face is weeping
and the eyes gone astray

   you do this!
   do it!
   lead me astray

# CABIN

*"too atomized to make pleasure of melancholy"*

## True Story Of The Pool

It was so hot although I didn't have much time I went to the pool. It was crowded — mostly with a group of Spanish-speaking youths. I figured they were from Colombia or Venezuela and decidedly upper class, as they spoke with Castilian accents. They were probably exchange students at the University. I was feeling tired, sluggish and "out of shape."

The boys were smoking cigarettes, which is really irritating when you poke your head out of water gasping for air, and one of them had a cassette machine blaring some abominable international Latinesque disco music. Nevertheless I plunged into the pool splashed about then retreated to a light green metal chaise lounge across from them to sun.

I had a huge callus on my big toe and couldn't refrain from picking at it — casually at first and then more and more ferociously until I could no longer contain the overwhelming urge to bite the thing off and did exactly that. I drew my foot up to my mouth and chomped on the callus. At this point one of the youths broke out in Spanish:

> "Sí, sí, damas y caballeros! Acerquese al circo, para ver la dama que se muerde el pie propio!"

> (Yes, yes, step right up to the circus, ladies and gentlemen, and see the lady who eats her own foot!)

I was amused myself but stood up defiantly, glaring at them all and donned my enormous grey parachute pants.

"And, she lives in a sack!" they all chorused uproariously.

## Cabin

eviction people arrive to haunt me
    with descriptions of summer's wildflowers
        how they are carpet of fierce colors

I bet you hate to see us they say and yes
    I do hate to have to move again especially from here
        destruction brought to place of love

the uneven smiles that win she's a business woman
    blond tints that glow at sunset as profits rise
        alas what labor I employ

but to ensure a moment's joy
    sets branches trembling & arms chilled
        dear one long returning home, come to

clammy feverish details, muffed sorrow
    I turn to throw a tear of rage in the pot
        never remorse but hint of scruples I'd hope for

it is error it is speculation it is real estate
    it is the villain and comic slippery words
        the work of despotic wills to make money

I scream take it take your money! make your money
    go on it's only money, here's a wall of dry rot
        here's an unfinished ceiling, just a little sunlight

peeks through this dark, no luminance! exquisite St. Etienne
    stove doesn't work icebox either too hot or frozen
        firescreen tumbling down

kitchen insulation droops is ugly & a mess
    ah but love it here, only surface appearances
        to complain of, nothing does justice

to shape of actual events I love
    but a fight against artificiality
        its inherent antagonism, bald hatred of moving

and problem of thirsty fig tree in Burroughs
    apartment wakes me I don't want to go down there yet
        & how to orchestrate the summer properly

the problem of distress & not deriving pride from it
    too atomized to make pleasure of melancholy
        & an uncontrollable enthusiasm for throne & altar

I want to sit high want simple phalanx
    of power independent of everything but free will
        & one long hymn in praise of the cabin!

it is a confession in me impenetrably walled in
    like aesthetics like cosmos an organ of
        metaphysics and O this book gives me a headache

dear Weston La Barre let's have an argument
    because I see too clearly how rational I must be
        & the kernel of my faith corrupted

because you have no reliance on the shaman & outlaw
    or how depth of mind might be staggering
        everywhere except in how important science is

science? no he won't be fooled by visions
    whereas I wait for dazzling UFOs they announce
        will arrive high in these mountains

I repair the portal even invite stray horses in
    have a little toy receiving station
        that sits by the bed

at the edge of night all thoughts to place of love
    all worries to this place of love
        all gestures to the place of love

all agonies to place of love, thaws to place
    of love, swarthy valley sealed
        in wood, log burst into flame

100

in home of love, all heart's dints and
　　machinations, all bellows & pungency
　　　　antemundane thoughts to palace of love

all liberties, singularity, all imaginings
　　I weep for, Jack's sweet almond-eyed daughter to
　　　　place of love, & heavy blankets

and terracing & yard work & patch work
　　& tenacity & the best in you
　　　　surround me work in me to place my love

dear cirques, dear constraint, dissenting
　　inclinations of a man and a woman, Metonic cycle
　　　　all that sweats in rooms, lives in nature

requiems & momentum & trimmings of bushes
　　dried hibiscus & hawks & shyness
　　　　brought to this place of love

trees rooted fear rooted all roots brought
　　to place of love, mystery to heart of love
　　　　& fibers

and fibers in sphere of love a whole world makes
　　spectators of slow flowering of spring
　　　　& summer when you walk to town for eggs

and continuous hammerings as new people
　　arrive & today we notice for first time
　　　　a white-crowned sparrow out by the feeder

with the chickadees & juncos & I missed
　　that airplane-dinosaur in dream nervous
　　　　to travel again, miss buds pop open

to shudder in breeze, their tractability
　　makes sudden rise of sensibility you are
　　　　shuddering too & your boy laugh

comes less frequent now you're drawn into
        accountability, will I return to find all
                stuff tidy in silver truck

ready to go? it's you in this place I lose
        most because it's here in you I forget
                where I am, this place for supernaturals

perched high in sky & wind, held by wind in stationary
        motion as bluebird we observe over meadow or caught
                up with jetstream dipping in valley's soft cradle

power & light & heat & radiance of head it takes
        power & light & heat & radiance of head it takes to
                make it work while

down there someone building replicas of what
        it feels like to be a human multitude, fantasy
                molded clumsily, spare my loves

and love of glorious architecture when you really put
        outside in, the feeling of cloud or mountain
                or stone

having developed an idea of idyllic private life
        & sovereignty of spirit over common
                empirical  demand

I tell you about renunciation, I tell you holy
        isolation like a river nears ocean to
                dissolve

and cabin becomes someone's idea of a good place
        discretion you pay for it wasn't mine either
                but sits on me imprints on me

forever splendor of fog, snow shut strangers out
        gradual turn of season, ground stir, pine
                needle tickle your shoulder, peak curve, fresh air.

# FIRST BABY POEMS

*"tossed as boat or cloud, gravid"*

Languor, uselessness & general swamp I'd be or
   am proclivity to lie down, catch how
   certainly large I'm being, more food to
   hungry belly-dweller, conversant in
   lambent things, long talk, room for
   growing feet, infant cloth feet, animal
   feet or simply sing about the animals,
   naming their delicate

Suede buttresses: buttes, metamorphic rocks,
   gravidly mesozoic. Stages of all you
   could ever be: tadpole, butterfly
   (Colorado marble or Alexandra's sulphur),
   fish (rainbow trout, squawfish, northern
   sucker), reptile (western skink), spadefoot
   toad, rufous-sided towhee I can't go on
   indefinitely listing but also include
   tender plants in a fertile

Soup. Also imagine the tree of vessels in
   placenta, the yolk sac, pale anemic
   vesicle under amnion, subcutis, corium,
   sebaceous glands, maxilla, at this stage:
   fish or frog or young bird. It
   flutters but never flies away. 8/9 of
   the way through it's a luminous,
   kicking, spiky, weighty, hiccupping
   roving traveler.

## Song: Time Drawes Neere

Time drawes neere
    love adornes you
        pours down autumn sunne

Babye I follow you
    sweete offspringe of
        nighte & sleepe

Pangs of the babye
    tossed in a bellie:
        birdies & woodland cheer!

Eies gaze with delighte
    I hope I fear I laugh
        call you "rolling mountain"

Your roote is deepe, be you englishe
    rosie fayre or german darkly
        call you boy or girl?

I must have pillows & musicke
    I must have raspberry leaf tea
        I needs must groan Ah me!

Ah thee! a secret growing
    I go no more a-maying
        I settle into my tent shift

Bursting at seams
    big tub, water barrel
        tossed as boat or cloud, gravid

Powre to claime my hart in
    bodye roome, powre to keepe
        me waking all nighte a-peeing

I ride you unseene wave
    wee rise together
        under daddye's roof & hand.

## Number Song

I've multiplied, I'm 2.
He was part of me,
he came out of me,
he took a part of me.
He took me apart.
I'm 2, he's my art,
no, he's separate.
He art one. I'm not
done & I'm still one.
I sing of my son. I've
multiplied.  My heart's
in 2, half to him &
half to you,
who are also a part
of him, & you & he
& I make trio of
kind  congruity.

## Scallop Song

I wore a garland of the briar that put me now in awe

I wore a garland of the brain that was whole

It commanded me, done babbling

And I no more blabbed, spare no lie

Tell womanhood she shake off pity

Tell the man to give up tumult for the while

To wonder at the sight of baby's beauty

Ne let the monsters fray us with things that not be

From a high tower poem issuing

Everything run along in creation till I end the song

Ne none fit for so wild beasts

Ne none so joyous, ne none no give no lie

Tell old woes to leave off here:

I sing this into a scallop shell with face of a pearl

& leave all sorrow bye & bye.

## Complaynt

*after Emily Dickinson*

I'm wanton — no I've stopped that,
That old place
I've changed, I'm Mother
It's more mysterious.
How odd the past looks
When I reread old notebooks,
See their faces fade
I feel it everywhere
& ordinary too
Am I safer now?
Was other way gayer?
I'm Mother now, O help &
Continue!

## Baby's Pantoum

### for Reed


I lie in my crib midday this is
        unusual I don't sleep really
Mamma's sweeping or else boiling water for tea
        Other sounds are creak of chair & floor, water
        dripping on heater from laundry, cat licking itself

Unusual I don't sleep really
        unless it's dark night everyone in bed
Other sounds are creak of chair & floor, water
dripping on heater from laundry, cat licking itself
        & occasional peck on typewriter, peck on my cheek

Unless it's dark night everyone in bed
        I'm wide awake hungry wet lonely thinking
occasional peck on typewriter, peck on my cheek
        My brain cells grow, I get bigger

I'm wide awake wet lonely hungry thinking
        Then Mamma pulls out breast, says "Milky?"
My brain cells grow, I get bigger
        This is my first Christmas in the world

Mamma pulls out breast, says "Milky?"
        Daddy conducts a walking tour of house
This is my first Christmas in the world
        I study knots in pine wood ceiling

Daddy conducts a walking tour of house
        I study pictures of The Madonna del Parto, a
        sweet-faced Buddha & Papago Indian girl
I study knots in pine wood ceiling
        I like contrasts, stripes, eyes & hairlines

I study pictures of The Madonna del Parto, a
sweet-faced Buddha & Papago Indian girl
        Life is colors, faces are moving

I like contrasts, stripes, eyes & hairlines
        I don't know what I look like

Life is colors, faces are moving
        They love me smiling
I don't know what I look like
        I try to speak of baby joys & pains

They love me smiling
        She takes me through a door, the wind howls
I try to speak of baby joys & pains
        I'm squinting, light cuts through my skin

She takes me through a door, the wind howls
        Furry shapes & large vehicles move close
I'm squinting, light cuts through my skin
        World is vast I'm in it with closed eyes

Furry shapes & large vehicles move close
        I rest between her breasts, she places me on dry leaves
World is vast I'm in it with closed eyes
        I'm locked in little dream, my fists are tight

I rest between her breasts, she places me on dry leaves
        He carries me gently on his chest & shoulder
I'm locked in little dream, my fists are tight
        They showed me moon in sky, was something
        in my dream

He carries me gently on his chest & shoulder
        He calls me sweet baby, good baby boy
They showed me moon in sky, was something
in my dream
        She is moving quickly & dropping things

He calls me sweet baby, good baby boy
        She sings hush go to sleep right now
She is moving quickly & dropping things
        They rock my cradle, they hold me tightly in their arms

She sings hush go to sleep right now
        She wears red nightgown, smells of spice & milk
They rock my cradle, they hold me tightly in their arms
        I don't know any of these words or things yet

She wears a red nightgown, smells of spice & milk
        He has something woolen and rough on
I don't know any of these words or things yet
        I sit in my chair & watch what moves

He has something woolen & rough on
        I can stretch & unfold as he holds me in the bath
I sit in my chair & watch what moves
        I see when things are static or they dance

I can stretch & unfold as he holds me in the bath
        Water is soft I came from water
I can see when things are static or they dance
        like flames, the cat pouncing, shadows or light
        streaming  in

Water is soft I came from water
        Not that long ago I was inside her
like flames, the cat pouncing, shadows or light
streaming  in
        I heard her voice then I remember now

Not that long ago I was inside her
        I lie in my crib midday this is
always changing, I am expanding toward you
        Mamma's sweeping or else boiling water for tea.

## Napping in the Shadow of Day

The house is still that shook with glee
Where did it go?
The shades pulled down
No one to phone
Silence the music, the clock
Baby is sleeping like a locket
His body ran down
Hush when you visit
Don't knock nor fidget
The day sits waiting
You must too
Hush he's lightly breathing

## Baby & the Gypsy

Wizened elf woman
crouched over sink
in ladies' room
at O'Hare Airport
looks up, sees us
in mirror, her eyes wide

> —Oh a baby!
> Let me hold the baby
> You take your time, dearie

She holds him like an icon
while I wash my face

> —He's got a future, this one
> He'll break some hearts
> Don't you worry about that!

## Mother & Child

*after Carew*

Child:      What is the destination of the sunlight's
            particles?

Mother:     Your hair, of course. Atoms of light created
            for your beauty, your beauty's articles

Child:      And where do roses go when they fade?

Mother:     Into your beauty, where they sleep in the
            shade

Child:      And where does the nightingale fly when
            she stops singing?

Mother:     Into your mouth where she continues
            singing until the seasons come round again

Child:      And what about the falling stars, where do
            they go?

Mother:     Into your eyes where they twinkle, as if
            you didn't know

Child:      And where goes the Phoenix, that magical
            bird which alternately burns and rises from
            its own ashes?

Mother:     It builds its nest of immortality upon your
            little breast, my child, under your innocent
            lashes

# MAKEUP ON EMPTY SPACE

*"Ripe palm age to come so wise to words"*

## Some of the Things I See for You

1

Great & dramatic he is sprouting a truant
officer who's caught the kid (ram)
I watch Balzac light his candelabra
Or missed the kid she was gone so long
Ram against heart. That's funny
I am sometimes that child. Balzac
take your bath now
It's evening. Jupiter hangs in the north
east window
A western concert of cars below Jupiter
above the ground 5 floors now spend
the time shining dimes
or spend them quickly before they lose
value, car saddened by the bash

I want you to walk in late like the German
director into his own movie
                                        pierce my heart
lie down beside the insect & sleep
or stop the fuss of beautiful evaporated birds


2

This is the luxury of February
& the ease of language that grows
on the 6 window sills
green language or language of sun, cloud language
or language of bird
if seeing were the lighting I think it is.
Language, you are the glittering treasures locked in
the drawer he is pulling open to get the whole
thing started
& we two live only to love that moment
they're found

            Treasures of time
the wind sends you down the mountain to gather
remember? Remember the way it smelled

your hand? & lift this one up to the light
to get a better look

I've mixed in the morning while you sleep
in a room like Paris the country
it's a capricious morning bath
not unlike the back of the mind
               perpetual & cloudy water

I wonder about the dolphin who danced
my part
when I dreamed that I slept & dreamed
that I dreamed
you are everywhere persuasive
                  dazzling sun moaning in my past

## Matriarchly

I GAVE THIS PART AWAY FROM ME

& does it come back to me does it does it. Does the man have
a heart, does he, and is it calling. It is if it is calling.
I gave this part away from me and does it come back to me does
it does it. June 1975 October Nineteen Seventy-Five January
1976 February Nineteen Seventy Six February Nineteen Hundred
and Seventy Seven and April 1977 and the summer, does it come
back to you does it does it. Does the man have a heart. Does
he. Does he. Does the man have a heart and is it calling. It
is if it is calling.

                2 others.

A letter writing woman takes this all down in memory. She does
and spell the gnomic imagery of Emily Dickinson mending chairs.

She knows how to wicker.
She raises cane.
Calliope, muse of epic poetry.

Does she have a heart now does she does she and does it come back
to me does it does it. It does and it is calling.

                I had my house
                it burned to shreds
                I picked me up
                & off I sped

                        long enough to leave a light
purple in hue
            The Clairvoyant said about not meeting this lifetime
again: you are purple with a circle of yellow

Does it come back to me now does it does it.

Spruce, Euclid, Grant Place, then Magnolia, Chautauqua, Caribou
Beaver Valley Estates, the birthdays of Independence, Dick Gallup,
Simone, Frank O'Hara. Larry, Peter Orlovsky.

Before that the birthday of Steven Fog the Eleventh of April.
The Alexandrian Geometrician c. 300 B.C.

      making this a suspended rhyme, a contained rhyme
         it is the same        it is articulate

         and does it come back to me
         does it       does it

(little Michael come out and play)

& there's a monk's hood chivalry to be seen in this not so
crowded valley in order the sky makes or mountain weather
as in O yes I remember mountain weather it's so variable
it's so variable as she's moody or quick or something
fast repartee, Gregory
                Gregory the Gargoyle
to be seen at certain hours, the wrath or flame or some such

      I like the Permian Period for its mountains not its reptiles

I'm fire. Got fire. Will be fire. Was fire and I was ashes too.

& does it come back to you does it does it
does the man have a heart does he does he

         little flowers little purple shooting star
           a bit of yellow

           a creature dependent on another: You
        I say it's you

thank you for taking me to the grove and pointing them out

these Libras, these liberties, these you take nicely along
and O

            I see Mountainly
                        and from an island, Manhattanly
& in my heart, Matriarchly

so it's a tract elevated to the point of outstanding
melodies of all the ones you'd ever hope to hear, that is,
human

                        & does it come back to me does it does it

Heh mother's got salve
mother's got away to go
mother's a sacristy
mother keep the germs away
protect me, mother
your little angel with cunt wings
mother, a big brain
mother, smarter than the baby girl
mother, I must complete my solo
mother, I rebuff you
mother, I adore you
you're my true lover, mother, never fear
mother, I know I scowl I
don't mean to
see the starkness of morning, mother!
smell the sweet alyssum
here's my comely man to meet you
here's my lovely lady to see you
mother, the clams are all female
here's my saline self to mix with you
we're autochthonous
we're gathering wool
we're weaving a garment
we're very sophisticated
we don't need a tryout
we're combing the beach now
we're fixed stars we're binary stars
you're standing over me
you're standing behind me
you're standing by me
you're at me feet

you be my moon you be my
tormentor you howl at me
you lock me in my room
you keep me wise
you be my milk, my book
my tigress, my sparrow hawk, my steed
you correcting me with soft eyes
bright lipstick in snappy brown suit
color of honey

(eight-year-old  memory)

    and does it come back
    does it

    does she have a heart
    does she & is it calling
       it is if it is calling

but a time in which she felt she'd gained some insight
into her feeling for X

      it got deranged
   was damaged, sent back
    editing was a long task
      laughter around a New Year
     it  superceded
        so & so got trendy
 slips away . . .

    the poet accompanied the musicians
the double rainbow outside hospital for Billy Burroughs, Jr.
    the sneak-about way of hotel life

Desk? this is the DESK speaking

your time is NOT up yet

    a fanfare for His Holiness
insane digressions all over my face
    insignias,  banners

developing a caste of dignity

the caste of Mabel Loomis Todd after Austin Dickinson died
　　　　　Jane Austen, Mansfield Park

writing in this wrought crystal of silence

send up some ice for my tequila
　　& for the baby boy:

Learn, babe, to laugh when Mother chides thee now,
Mother weary with her nine long months

Learn, babe, to laugh when Mother calls thee now,
Mother pale with her nine long months

Learn, babe, now: who answers not the smile of Mother's eyes
He is not meet to share a goddess's bed or table of a god

Learn, babe, to sing when Mother calls thee
Mother happy her nine long months are o'er

Learn, babe, thy Father's voice calling you now
Relieving Mother her long long months

Learn, babe, that life is sweet & suffering long
& blessings come from Father & Mother now

Learn, babe, to sing and laugh & be what fits a man
when you grow long years from now

& does it come back to me does it does it
does she say it does she does she
& is she saying it she is

　　　　　does he come back to himself
　　　　　　　does he does it come back to him
　　　　　　　　does it does it

does he come back to himself does he does he

does it happen like this

    dozing off and falling asleep to dreams
        one summer night:

and these are the dreams one summer night:

1. Terry Cloth Man says she's in there in shower she's not snot
but comes to my side like a miniature Bianca intent to leave
intending to leave little twin girl to leave, going to Phila
Delf    IA   will take maybe 10 maybe 20 hours

    A place of Oracles

A Man Who Speaks Between He's All Breathing He's a Go-Between

Intending upon Elfia intent upon a city
        palace of Oracles

I've pulled her down on me she's incredible oriental hair
& white skin

        whoosh

suffer sufficiently she says she has to      half to

I drive away in the big truck in the brilliantine

Frozen  Albania

Wrong lane in the Holy Straightway Truck & suddenly
it's a starry murder blocking the road

    the murder of Om Mani

Om Mani Padme Hum

        Old Man you keep holding yr back
        Old Man you keep holding back
        & strolling down the road

slits open, Women Who See Matriarchly

2. The Vulcan Poets Anthology: I can't get beyond the title on
the Award-Winning poet's metal shelf—Each book's got a gate
around it
              books of firebrand meteors   the Revulsion Poets
the Poets at the Gates of Hell?
                                  Gate gate parasamgate
                    the Vulva Can Poets?

I think: so many monster cunts to be written

3. Dream "Wolverine" comes before "Woman" in the dictionary

perfunctory & true

giddyup giddyup

4. My Dandy Son "Robbins" is turning into the 17th century
I've just give painful birth & he's growing younger
something about Skylab & you're an old lady now

All the stars nodding for the mother of the Dandy

     does she come back to you does she does she
          & is she saying it    she is

 and does he come back to himself does he does he
does the man have a heart and is it calling
     it is if it is calling

so it's a tract elevated and never to be forgotten going on
& on like a point of view, seeing cinematically now

          I GAVE THIS PART AWAY FROM ME & DOES IT COME BACK TO ME
               DOES IT DOES IT

& here's the final birdlike dream to find my way:

Last night I dream my bones are hollow
I can fly down the avenues

At Houston & Sixth the widow

Von Behr & her daughter swoon
falling like rubber to the ground
inky shadows stretch out before them
under the bright moon

My mother steals ahead with my coat
Houston is lined with amusements
In one house the Rossetti sisters
fumigate the room where
the sea captain has died

In another, men sit with their sons
at picnic tables & there's a comedy
about Africa being played in the hallway
further back

I fly down my childhood street
with swift bird anatomy
Mother turns the corner &
the moon goes out
I peck at the enormous switch
to bring it on again

## Two Hearts

*after Sir Philip Sidney*

She's got my heart and I've got hers
It was fair, we fell in love
I hold hers precious and mine she would miss
There never was anything like this
Her heart in my brain keeps us one
My heart in her guides thoughts and feelings
She loves my heart for once it was hers
I love hers because it lived in me
I once wounded her, it was misunderstanding
And then my heart hurt for her heart
For as from me on her her hurt did sit
So I felt still in me her hurt hurt, it
Both of us hurt simultaneously and then we saw how
We're stuck with each other's hearts now.

## Dialogue Between the Self & the Soul

SOUL:
Within your delight I'm warm, exquisite, take pride
in your scale, every interval, no oblique approaches,
and thus have power to float above the walls, appear
in tragic focus or not, and as it suits our mutual potency
not reduce the strain of living double in the world
The hero, the student, the mistress, the actress, the diplomat
was my life also, and mocked the steady running of the hour
Was my life also, and dreamt no love goes lagging.

SELF:
But what of love? You know how Dante meets the souls of
Paolo and Francesca in the second ring of hell, how they
are borne along on the dim infernal wind because they loved
too hotly in the flesh, you know how Francesca, the once
happy girl of Rimini, remembers the coherence of 3-dimensional
space and the ecstatic hours of her earthly lust and how
Dante must pause at her compassionate speech of adultery to weep.
Such, not us, reflect and have the day, let them wail!

SOUL:
And well they might. He uses it. How passion took the
color of their faces as she read to him of the love of
Lancelot, how Paolo kissed her mouth all trembling.
The poet never questions the judgement that puts them there
but feels human pity nonetheless and desire to include
them in his divine poem in sweet flaming glory.
The soul shall never be cut into, the self shall
always have that wandlike presence and use it. You use me.

SELF:
And you don't mind, for experience is always double. And
there are two ways of knowing—by argument and by
experience. How can you argue fire burns without
experiencing it? The imagination leaps around flamboyant
curves (especially in love) and glances through thin stone
armatures—diagonally, vertically, horizontally. In
this environment the figure, unless emancipating itself
from the control of the wall, will never view the fire.

SOUL:

This is true, and experience tells us lovers float like
rain. They drop their nets and walk into the wall like
smoke. Ancient women smile. Ordinary people are peculiar
too. There is something about love in all of this and
mere motion. I'm here because it's been required, there
is no argument. I crash around the bend and beat for
light as you do. I join myself to the great rapt silence
or soar when you do.

## Sisters

First make the mouthpiece classic
so that my passionate Spanish sister
will take some lessons        Take her out of hand
& blow her into the palm of the world
Put a date into the palm of the world

     It's her birthday

Ripe palm age to come so wise to words

It needn't be a question of how handsome she is

Accept the apologies of the sisters

              *

Sister Solitude has another sister
whose got a punch you won't forget
or move into until earth abandons mitts
to summer        Summer gives a fast speech
covering the earth with a plan

One descends from the mirror to take the prize
another sends out a message to resemble youth

       waddling away

             *

They are my sisters both        Since he is not
sufficiently paid attention to
let him go out the door backwards
my sisters say
They are so cruel

## Makeup on Empty Space

I am putting makeup on empty space
all patinas convening on empty space
rouge blushing on empty space
I am putting makeup on empty space
pasting eyelashes on empty space
painting the eyebrows of empty space
piling creams on empty space
painting the phenomenal world
I am hanging ornaments on empty space
gold clips, lacquer combs, plastic hairpins on empty space
I am sticking wire pins into empty space
I pour words over empty space, enthrall the empty space
packing, stuffing jamming empty space
spinning necklaces around empty space
Fancy this, imagine this: painting the phenomenal world
bangles on wrists
pendants hung on empty space
I am putting my memory into empty space
undressing you
hanging the wrinkled clothes on a nail
hanging the green coat on a nail
dancing in the evening it ended with dancing in the evening
I am still thinking about putting makeup on empty space
I want to scare you: the hanging night, the drifting night,
the moaning night, daughter of troubled sleep I want to scare you
you
I bind as far as cold day goes
I bind the power of 20 husky men
I bind the seductive colorful women, all of them
I bind the massive rock
I bind the hanging night, the drifting night, the
moaning night, daughter of troubled sleep
I am binding my debts, I magnetize the phone bill
bind the root of my pointed tongue
I cup my hands in water, splash water on empty space
water drunk by empty space
Look what thoughts will do   Look what words will do
from nothing to the face

from nothing to the root of the tongue
from nothing to speaking of empty space
I bind the ash tree
I bind the yew
I bind the willow
I bind uranium
I bind the uneconomical unrenewable energy of uranium
dash uranium to empty space
I bind the color red I seduce the color red to empty space
I put the sunset in empty space
I take the blue of his eyes and make an offering to empty space
renewable blue
I take the green of everything coming to life, it grows &
climbs into empty space
I put the white of the snow at the foot of empty space
I clasp the yellow of the cat's eyes sitting in the
black space I clasp them to my heart, empty space
I want the brown of this floor to rise up into empty space
Take the floor apart to find the brown,
bind it up again under spell of empty space
I want to take this old wall apart I am rich in my mind thinking
of this, I am thinking of putting makeup on empty space
Everything crumbles around empty space
the thin dry weed crumbles, the milkweed is blown into empty space
I bind the stars reflected in your eye
from nothing to these typing fingers
from nothing to the legs of the elk
from nothing to the neck of the deer
from nothing to porcelain teeth
from nothing to the fine stand of pine in the forest
I kept it going when I put the water on
when I let the water run
sweeping together in empty space
There is a better way to say empty space
Turn yourself inside out and you might disappear
you have a new definition in empty space
What I like about impermanence is the clash
of my big body with empty space
I am putting the floor back together again
I am rebuilding the wall
I am slapping mortar on bricks

I am fastening the machine together with delicate wire
There is no eternal thread, maybe there is thread of pure gold
I am starting to sing inside about the empty space
there is some new detail every time
I am taping the picture I love so well on the wall:
moonless black night beyond country-plaid curtains
everything illuminated out of empty space
I hang the black linen dress on my body
the hanging night, the drifting night, the moaning night
daughter of troubled sleep
This occurs to me
I hang up a mirror to catch stars, everything occurs to me out in the
night in my skull of empty space
I go outside in starry ice
I build up the house again in memory of empty space
This occurs to me about empty space
that it is nevered to be mentioned again
Fancy this
imagine this
painting the phenomenal world
there's talk of dressing the body with strange adornments
to remind you of a vow to empty space
there's talk of the discourse in your mind like a silkworm
I wish to venture into a not-chiseled place
I pour sand on the ground
Objects and vehicles emerge from the fog
the canyon is dangerous tonight
suddenly there are warning lights
The patrol is helpful in the manner of guiding
there is talk of slowing down
there is talk of a feminine deity
I bind her with a briar
I bind with the tooth of a tiger
I bind with my quartz crystal
I magnetize the worlds
I cover myself with jewels
I drink amrita
there is some new detail
there is a spangle on her shoe
there is a stud on her boot
the tires are studded for the difficult climb

I put my hands to my face
I am putting makeup on empty space
I wanted to scare you with the night that scared me
the drifting night, the moaning night
Someone was always intruding to make you forget empty space
you put it all on
you paint your nails
you put on scarves
all the time adorning empty space
Whatever-your-name-is I tell you "empty space"
with your fictions with dancing come around to it
with your funny way of singing come around to it
with your smiling come to it
with your enormous retinue & accumulation come around to it
with your extras come round to it
with your good fortune, with your lazy fortune come round to it
when you look most like a bird, that is the time to come around to it
when you are cheating, come to it
when you are in your anguished head
when you are not sensible
when you are insisting on the
praise from many tongues
It begins with the root of the tongue
it begins with the root of the heart
there is a spinal cord of wind
singing & moaning in empty space

# Incantation

(SPHINX OF MY HEART GUESSED OUT OF DEPTH)

*for Frances LeFevre Waldman*


Light as motion, people flit lightly along
asphalt, mottled bud & bloom I saw covered shadow
of leaf & building, autumn shadows lengthening
looks this way wading across a path whose
shadow is one of shadowy, one of the

grey men pads himself in layers of cloth
charcoals face and hitchhikes up canyon, eyeing
phenomena with big fish glitter eye, other closed
into tiny fist, walking from food store may be
dangerous, serpentine, more druid, muddy

provocation say newspapers amongst street
people & local highschool now waving bats and knives,
make war-cries although today there's talk of truce
& questionnaire asks have you ever been harassed
on the mall? No, but never there at night,

rarely by day, as little as possible, seizure's
on me like exploding there's never enough of
that or money, there's grateful one, there's grateful
sum, some are grateful but get jittery here
something careless going on spending, & more

spending power in choices. Coloradan means
posture, means quick thundershower, means natural
beauty, means biosphere, pink cloud, means you have
accounts, means subsisting, means anonymous,
means notice young men support clay mask

replicas of sad beast face that lived in
deep past we've never articulated but now returning
soon like diviners or maybe I am fantasizing they are
buffers. It is Halloween sport to stop you on
street, shriek & flail, do impudent flip

Will slow down, will walk slow, will be slower
way coming home by bus unscathed with damaged
and handicapped who are like ferrets, responding as
if to say it's what we are, have dealings with,
blond and twisted and askew, able to shout

hello in all friendliness. There's contest for
sweetest bus driver this month I'll pick this one, she's
natural, punctual & new portent fills me with amaze
and blanch out thought, so sense of self ravished
sheepish and disconcerting, slim needing

vitamins! vitamins! drift your course between
attritions, something about a school I'm helping
run and dissolve. A bikeway is proposed intrusively
through bird sanctuary, it's continual battle
as if there must always be sides opposing

and assigned to seats too crowded if you
ask him he gives cynical reply I can't stand.
Can't stand if motorized or something can't truly
drive car yet or ever will get close and loving
to dashboard, its hue and collusion

Hard to play down, hard to be outstanding bill
outstanding model of the world in a house it is
quaint to be offhand, no longer staked or stalked like
figure of speech using will use always using have
been using and wanting to ameliorate

situation of dream people in a house waiting
for winter waiting for work waiting to make a slant
toward a city, any city where you could have sunshine
the way it's light here or airy way to be walking
under moon with no bones on tonight. I sleep

like a bird always ready to be gone. There's no
where to go leadenly, but all happening smoothly as trip
in straw vehicle imagined so we could feel the breeze
but city what city what pressure driven by more
urgent cares. Who's weeping, who's crazy now?

The movie sickens you because it repeats the
spry outcome of years of mistake like war, but then
intends it to be spirit of a decade, prime volition
to let all go off again, not sit down in one spot
to breathe out again. These are instructions:

We breathe some poison in on us, we breathe it out
transmuted in our mind. It is so, & dust of several
thousand centuries & accretions of hard heads & aggregates
of the part-woman who cried loudly & did
this to you, waving her arms & the earth rumbles

and you are her banner. And if I knew science
could tell you ramifications of mind, of thought that
arises never not too scared to do something with, I would
cheer. No one watching this but you old watcher and boot
you out & kill old thought, bury it. Morning

dawning in a look, anyone's. "In this direction came
a mind to me last night" & rise up condensed by cooler
weather coming on rapidly only recently we could say this
about weather hallooing the more because how talkative
it gets around a cloud and no issue but to tell you

what it is looking like when it looks good.
Resembles pulp, resembles a lake, resembles wind
whining or postman delivering letters. Sometimes it is
3 students coming up the walk, one is surely a lover
of beauty, and sometimes they resemble old lovers

or surveyors or survivors who left their implements
behind on the sand and never returned although they
knew the art of measuring with their bodies, it is their
duty. And they knew how to make skirts from the inner
bark of the cedar tree, how to oil their faces &

how to sing. Congruent, venturesome ideas of everyone
you've loved and known are consumed on the spot. Always
resisting this, spent hours at nothing particularly grand,
taking a rest, reading that day a chronicle and writing
down names over & over, ripped a letter, barred a door

put up drapes, sent rest away saying I will not I
cannot break this attention span, this ring, this utterance,
this scanning the sky as if it does come alive by itself and
talked down narrowly to a feather, spots on the wall
decorating a place you try to convert. It does come

alive of itself. My green pen, my hard chair, the
materials of one's trade you can't exactly call attention
to what's around and tell you pretty sheets it's like
morning when you glow and say things that are so
knowingly slipping away in intensity, gorgeous

glittering objects. See them bounce on walls. But
to build a town is not the answer being so stubborn of
head and growing up wrong in daylight not that you did but
some perversity makes you laugh, toss care behind you
not a founding father though you'd never be content

in hours spent dreaming, coming away from mimeo
machine more filmy, maybe forlorn as job gets
done, pages congeal in apprehension of winter you haven't
quite thawed since last, more work, more disasters:
the prostitutes of Denver refuse to serve Iranian

customers in their bodies, they make a statement
they can't tell an Arab from an Iranian although
they will lose money on this deal it is conscience.
Grocery store man says it's a mistake to think most
of the 500 Iranians living in this city would

even frequent a house of ill repute and the
pimp is extremely self-righteous and now some bit
of violence everywhere around this, you see how endless
is the hatred when it gets placed in the heart
so willful, arrogant, gluts the stage

extraneous, indignities of generalization,
cartoon of horror, tower of pride, unmanageable,
unnecessary, extrinsic, mirror images of hate, envy,
territoriality, all hideous things are exhausting,
miserable, morbid, stubborn, nothing is bending

137

I won't remember any of these qualities. Some of
the town is reflecting light off her mountains tonight.
Remember about the unidentified objects chasing the Spanish
plane. It landed in Tenerife, properly tentative
nobody wants them, to lend them a reef, they might

be hostile, strange. They are, as is the hole
in the sound of the record, the man making a hole on
the red sofa, or animal at the door wanting to be in to
be eating wanting some pleasure. I was thinking of
the friend of mine who is troubled the most, who

favors subjugation to authority to breathing free,
& sits in hospitals and how I would say when I get
the nerve Are you seeing what you are hating what you are
hungry for, what you sleep to cover and how you are
locked in your dailiness and do you ever want to

change it around? Probably not. Then fertile &
enchanting Haydn was performed. I thought the pianist
was going to break the bench he was leaping so hard,
childlike in his bouncy flesh, ovate, precise, virtuous
in his rendering of *Gaspard de la Nuit.* I was

wondering if the Cubans sitting in front of me with
mustaches were there because they like music or because he
was Cuban. They walked out at the end like soldiers. How
we are continually taking the trouble to pass these things
composed for the instrument down through briny ages

when it is motion & designed for involvement, you
listen in on display of fusion, sometimes amnesia of body,
tones groaning, fingers skitter like a crab, you laugh,
whole thing swaying not resolved you are in a flurry
& it will go on & on, everyone is clapping

& running to cars in cold. Why do the newspapers
confuse a few with a whole people? Why a whole people
with a few? It is costing the present administration no
small difficulty, they will not be victorious of heart
in the next election although on the other hand, I could

never vote for a person who makes you culpable if
you drive a friend to demonstration at nuclear trigger warhead
plant even if you aren't participating, and if you are of
course it is even worse, drum roll so he's out, there
is no bargain, there is no slippery deal

I can only offer the Symphony no.103 in E-flat Major
to this current problem and the beauty of the state I live
in, watching jagged "Irons" we call them this morning in their
glory looking like new islands jutting from a bed of
whitecaps, new continent forming, thrusting into

gauzy blue, it is meeting of certain qualities
both just-born and youthful, they patch up rip I was
seeing in the sky last night, murder heard about, gaping
hole of ugliness and misery which fills corners & edges
of house with tears, so many of them

Martha Braun is dead. Clouds like beads strung
across peaks now, everyone out playing as if pretty
day beckoned. It did, Sierra & Naomi roll down hill
in backyard in a plastic bucket, amber leaves
stubbornly clutch onto branches

sun is down you know there's hot food everywhere
on a table in this town and indoors is still crowded
with everything you left unattended before you went out,
a piece of paper reminds you to do something soon, her
address, other stacks of paper to be put between

covers when it was a plain when it was a desert
when it was paradisiacal when it was before it was recycling
when it had wild sage everywhere, when it trembled in wind,
and deer were nearer nibbling. We take old phonebooks
and newspapers to the recycling trailer

1 lb. of aluminum cans is worth 22 cents whereas the
equal amount of glass is only half a penny. Thinking
about what is indestructible makes my teeth shiver as if I'd
have to eat nails, swallow chemicals, live in fire, walk
on coals, run huge distances, never sleep

The persistent realm of molten steel all the notes
plunged into abyss you couldn't hear them ever again all
the chlorine leaking from derailments, people evacuated,
harder to be alive in fragility in a body in a chemistry
in a world, in a tourniquet in a splint

in a change between unions and management. Nuggets
were tied with Lakers and clearly through tomorrow night
cloudy on Sunday if you want it and brought to you by
Western Federal Savings branches in Colorado, all inviting
you into their buildings, all saying the same thing

about money: keep it in the bank otherwise it melts
out there with the snow! It's dusty, useless, it's no
fun, too saintly, like I would be saying something obsolete
so recent and callow to think it all, no I never had any
sense about money so when someone able to say that city

you lived in based purely on economy I was laughing
to spend it into the ground, topple over when everyone
gets so much at once, all have the same denominator, nothing
changes your friends just as nervous and strange what to
do with it, everyone in a soup, a spiral

Live, write gloriously, retreat into mountain air,
into mouth, into breathing, you see in this so-called
practice what you do is focus on your outbreath with your
mind and with your mind boycott the inbreath, gap
out dissolve, gap out dissolve

into little A-frame cabin like rocket & you are
worried outer space creatures will come & grab you in
your purity without recourse to telephone, you are in
complete isolation with stove, shrine, bed, dreams,
sweater, alphabet, candles, deities

Who is this woman prostrating herself in front of
what representation of her own mind, conjuring in her
mind images of all friends & relatives & enemies & sentience
for whom you prostrate saying I take you with me like
it or not, there is some memory of this

from past vision when I had similar picture under
drug not sure where to carry it, in front of what spot
and who is this running up hill and who is feeding carrots
to dapple horse and who is stoking the fire and who are
you lighting incense, then it curls: who are you?

No idols. I was in one mind of being a student, I
was in another mind of your lover, I was becoming
organized, I was the actress & diplomat, I was a reporter,
ambassador, hostess, traveler, singing for my supper
wearing warm boots, wrapped in wool, then sweating

I was smoky in the fire All Hallows' Eve. I
could hear coyotes howling, thought of dead stalking
about costumed, I took off all my clothes and bathed
with sponge in front of stove, flesh like candle wax
soon I would be melded into this place

turn into something that belongs here, cabin glowed
in kerosene, stove sounded like someone scraping &
breaking in a tin can, making fricatives, explosive
sound, so and so as a liquid offers no difficulty
moon was ringed with a rainbow of color

"What is written sweet sister on the door of this
legended tomb?" asks Poe addressing his soul Psyche,
her hair streaming in plantlike mystery, this image keeps
occurring to me like promise of things other than themselves
revealed, disquieting loneliness up here

miles above the sea, self-imposed isolation
not literary convention not reckless but reciprocity
between the woman and her mind but enough of that largesse
of oxygen, nothing spectral but more like close shave
and then you get up, walk out door

grasp of territory arriving like shock troops you
hold ground, its precious form, its eroticism, its
obligations, its sense of duty that whole future is
in its hands, then arrives like grace of waves in
water, caprice is unpredictable, then everything

falls away: goodbye precious hands, precious feet,
goodby precious eyebrows & slanting eyes, goodbye
knees bending, goodby desk, goodbye books & papers,
farewell to all instruments of poetry, all sentiment,
fury goodbye, goodbye doing her apprenticeship

for life in the world, goodbye god, goodbye
firmament. There is some description needed here about
sound of voices, how they are low & drawling: "western,"
broad, modest, inarticulate, everyone too
knocked out by vistas, as if speech could express

nothing at all but rather let us speak. We speak
through car horns, through radios, machines of any
kind, and though there's limit to how high you can go
there is building always going on, more fresh logs.
Woman walks into hardware store looks at some fake

walnut paneling, announces she's going to build a
house. This artificial stuff resembles jerky, then man
on corner of Aurora & 17th adds more cactus to his
already enormous cactus & rock garden, now like a
kingdom, building a bridge and a moat, soon it

conquers the street. 7 ravens in a tree as I turn
corner, they remind the street it's cold and winter.
Watch heavily made-up girl students buy overpriced shoes.
One named Olga with a large nose is fond of extremely
tall mauve spikes, open at the toe, other girl will

settle for any boot at all since she can't
have oyster, just so long it fits, her nailpolish
is the color of blood, she is almost Coloradan. More girls
buying boots like an initiation, rite of passage.
Fellow in Brillig Works shows me quote on blackboard

about sinking & swimming can you guess the famous
poet? Look at backs of trees, lose gloves, come
home to sew hole in pocket. More speckled or cleancut
day possibly, although air looks green over suburbs
of Denver, hedges more bleached, less people out

running. We parted on the corner and shook hands
"to sanity." I said he might be different than other
men here because he had look in his eye which reached
over them to the next place you could go. A slight
swagger was humbled, I liked him immediately he's

less dull. A wraithlike person sailed in in front
of the clerk, 3 borzois on a leash looked emaciated,
underfed but maybe they are supposed to be that way.
Quantities of good-naturedness don't have to lock your
heart up from your face but still uneasiness about

people in nonmoving vehicles when they are just
lingering there, always threatening like tank
commanders not out in the open enjoying the great day.
How it identifies with manhood, with dusk, atmosphere
permeates town, dogs in the back of pickup trucks

which is same feeling to be under spell, town exists
in bubble, we are breathing special air, growing more
radial, more plantlike. He steps out of a car now and walks
around to study his back fender, sensing my nervousness,
smiles sweetly the way you don't expect

precisely and now a more accurate view of November
like speaking of someone to reveal personal bias and
this a record of experience sometimes urgent sometimes just
natural movement of human feeling there is relief to
be alone in a love of elaboration. Couple

in a huddle, couple on the corner casually amiss,
uncommitted I'm thinking transient buying something slinky
while silver gliders patrol the skies, ostentatiously dip
like eccentric toys & clouds shift to form a kind of
curtain or screen or into shape of nerve endings,

one a charging gladiator, one an alligator which puts
me in mind to battle in which I would use my diamond
clamp as weapon, also my phurba, my crystal hook, my spear,
my moonstone fork, my love-knot, my defense, all of them:
the lasso, the whole team, the supernal ones!

Old men at Bill & Harold's Mobil station like grey
gnomes, faces hatcheted, smeared with grease, oddly
angelic, soft, no duplicity, not trying to put one over
we drive away with brand-new snow tires priced reasonably
one of the other small men having expounded on the

dangers of "re-caps" they won't get you through
more than a season, he said shaking genial or genie
head, nope, if that, it's a long season, chilled
now, wind in your ears, better do with thick
treads they're more secure (with a wink).

Sphinx of my heart guessed out of depth, elegance
is not all, the associations radiating from words of
everyday life, nothing done to them, direct contact with
experience, murmur of the mailman, he talks to his
radio, fussing or commenting on scores

There is needed proper chemistry of the team, city
of Denver suffering, someone's instinct for stillness,
another's for noise, another claims the ball, or maybe
like to think only of winning in the long practicings
no questions discussing radiation

and think not alone under the sun assumptions of
the 20th century, and play not for safety, for money
for glory, for revenge, but transmute rawness of your
time and feel alert, pointed impact of anything
painful. It feeds your vows, that vow to

contact experience with all wakefulness, go heedful
not in ease, not in bewilderment but attentive to
quality of night, queer blue sky, warm chinook, and hush
before dawn, examine those many colors and sunny
morns too, look at texture of mood before you

start dashing. No break in continuity of experience
no necessity but that of getting closer to momentary
passing of things: girl on skate, language of folded hands,
anything significant in how language is shifting, snow
on the porch swing, or language stretched

144

never remote never a gulf, rather capable of pleasure
not purely aesthetic pleasure but looking at the truth
in a bunch increasing susceptibility, urbanity, well-powdered
rational people, stick to it not succumb to restrictions
of night, bands of dark blue or grey

Intimacy of life spent quickening imagination, a
constancy to which a movie may aspire, poetry not always
polite you caution the reader, slip in some trimmings—
a rhapsody, good-natured condescension, the woman wants
to take you out of yourself, dazzle you

so you are new person when surrounded by something
you never saw before in nature: diction—how stretches
are punctuated by a fold, a dot of green held in brackets
by the altitude, a way that makes you shiver, not grand
design, I was just noticing . . .

I might borrow literally but there's no precedence
for what I might say about the West, too solemn tone,
never in danger of distorting shapeliness, don't want to
encourage inattention of reader to such peculiarities
as Astraspis which is primitive jawless fish of

Ordovician period from Canon City, one of the oldest
known fossil vertebrates. Rather I want to notice
amazonite, a green feldspar from Pikes Peak glittering
in moonlight, uplifts squeezing and pleating rocks
millions of years ago, then folds overturned

and split, cracks & faults permitted further
movement, erosion cut away mountains. Later regional
uplift with widespread volcanic action. Erosion continues,
rivers cut deeper gorges. Then as climate changed,
glaciers gorged the mountains, it isn't over yet

dramatic outline of peaks against the sky, panorama
of polished assemblies of rock, not ordinary common
sentiments, not ordinary common sediments disturbing my
sleep, interfering Jack says with his imagination,
nearly exasperating in splendid pride in purposeful

145

stance you can't equal that but in how you live your
whole life not platitudinously but who that person is
means you won't be straining. You knew where you were with
Pastoral, Elegy, Epic, the rest & it would take an
age to build this poem properly, so do it, start

now & be associated with Romanticism it dares you
here to spill over, ongoing & smartly spliced by time,
like you might be rolling tumbleweed. Does it squeeze
you, embrace you? Yes! It makes everything wonderfully
impossible and alien & close — separating a heart

from friends, lover, job, glimpse of deeper
possibility thinking you were mistaken it could
all be kept to surface, maybe you turn aside finally,
be just a visitor and the markings get thin, disappear
into drawings in the atlas, left behind, anyway

it's not about saving anyway, anyway what was it?
anyway can it support vanity? Anyway, locked in snow
storm falls charmingly discreetly 2 days make softer
world sharpen your eye, all cars wrapped up in white
snow blankets, gentler forms, more delicate for

senses, more constitutional, shapely, smooth
hulking trees, clumps like claws of the terrible
beast newly arrived from Arctic, no sound on ears, tumid
& gorgeous, benefit world with tender inclination
expressing lovely vision to open head who walks

in it, some are skiing too. What person gets
overemphatic in store but then turns friendly out-
side food stamp office, he listens patiently, not quite
hugging every little girl in sight, but then moves
visibly heavier by boots, by margin of behavior

you know he might still fall over on his face,
laughing, a truant, a rebel, gruff, not a bit tame,
adorned by two enormous dogs in back of a pickup that
that girl in the blond wig puts up with. Wish it
were clearer in its endlessness, some limitation

146

or restraint, all refined to moment she lifts her
head I can't get close enough now to green porcelain
lamp with embossed white leaves, large white cup reads
   "Enalc Hotel" like a tub, mottled in color of skin, scarf
      with colors of autumn Douglas sent in a German soap

      box, ivory-handled instrument for trim cuticles I've
   owned since age 10, more tearful objects and more
recent objects: large buckeye leaf, pebble from retreat
   in Livermore, button to convert Rocky Flats, inspirational
      picture of the Temple of Silence from Cave of the Winds

      with its helactites and pure calcite crystals, guidebook
   to Berlin, card depicting Memling's *Vision of St.*
*Jean* which includes a three-headed red dragon, a rainbow
   halo, a flaming boulder falling from sky to land on
      serene turquoise water, a winged horse. The saint

      sits on a mountain promontory pen & notebook in hand,
   wearing a pink dress. A little man in white shoots an
arrow. O vision of hell of fire of destruction of resurrection
   of human being writing it down of dragon head. We run to
      caves in this artistic sieve, is there circuit to your

      heart to your eye is it moving you toward your own
   version of world, without which complexity leads you
fully engaged, poet responds impulsively, special lion
   pride will lead you into a little cranny then later
      after period of solitude you are sought for out of

      this place. And who is watching thoughts who is
   checking the mailbox who is varied or modified tonight
who bounds across the yard whose eyes peer from lids and
   who takes your place when you drop fatigued and
      dream you are being rehearsed for an even

      larger speaking role? I would train to be able to
   die entering a dream and wake from dream into new
life and transfer consciousness too. Dear mother I hope
   this would interest you in your speculations not letting
      simplicity of style blind you to how it could be

147

grand thought or interesting architecture of mind.
And I would name all the parts of my body in their
language to put myself together again, and would list
the fir, spruce & pine of these parts, gathering
them to make a kingdom of two horizons, flat and

rocky, and would name all the mountain minerals to
make a chain with all the rivers, creeks & streams show
a map & collecting all the adventure & woe of people
who lived here once and currently write an epic and
with names of local birds such as grey-headed junco,

black-billed magpie, red-shafted flicker, Lincoln's
sparrow, belted kingfisher weave a blanket Coloradan
to include the names of tribes who flourished, and build an
incantation here where sky is never wholly empty
to hold the golden light of winter dusk.

148

# INVENTION

*"To make the energies dance etc."*

# A Phonecall from Frank O'Hara

*"That all these dyings may be life in death"*

I was living in San Francisco
My heart was in Manhattan
It made no sense, no reference point
Hearing the sad horns at night,
fragile evocations of female stuff
The 3 tones (the last most resonant)
were like warnings, haiku-muezzins at dawn
The call came in the afternoon
"Frank, is that really you?"

I'd awake chilled at dawn
in the wooden house like an old ship
Stay bundled through the day
sitting on the stoop to catch the sun
I lived near the park whose deep green
over my shoulder made life cooler
Was my spirit faltering, grown duller?
I want to be free of poetry's ornaments,
its duty, free of constant irritation,
me in it, what was grander reason
for being? Do it, why? (Why, Frank?)
To make the energies dance etc.

My coat a cape of horrors
I'd walk through town or
impending earthquake. Was that it?
Ominous days. Street shiny with
hallucinatory light on sad dogs,
too many religious people, or a woman
startled me by her look of indecision
near the empty stadium
I walked back spooked by
my own darkness
Then Frank called to say
"What? Not done complaining yet?
Can't you smell the eucalyptus,

have you never neared the Pacific?
'While frank and free /call for
musick while your veins swell'"
he sang, quoting a metaphysician
"Don't you know the secret, how to
wake up and see you don't exist, but
*that* does, don't you see phenomena
is so much more important than *this*?
I always love *that*."
"Always?" I cried, wanting to believe him
"Yes." "But say more! How can you if
it's sad & dead?" "But that's just it!
If! It isn't. It doesn't want to be
Do you want to be?" He was warming to his song
"Of course I don't have to put up with as
much as you do these days. These *years*.
But I do miss the color, the architecture,
the talk. You know, it *was* the life!
And dying is such an insult. After all
I was in love with breath and I loved
embracing those others, the lovers,
with my *body*." He sighed & laughed
He wasn't quite as I'd remembered him
Not less generous, but more abstract
Did he even have a voice now, I wondered
or did I think it up in the middle
of this long day, phone in hand now
dialing  Manhattan

# SKIN MEAT BONES

*"Of this you are understood, of measurement, of predicament."*

# I Digress . . .

It's something like the Merode altarpiece by Campin
at The Cloisters. Keep coming back to details.
Foreshadow being & doing in the world. The painting's
gratuitous, abstruse to most modern mortals.
Denaturation of words, fabricate upper panels, call it
cerebral, hermetic, religious, gleeful, laconic, sumptuous
& all the actions are involved in the paint: hatred
& love. I'm through with quarrels of salons, you
know how they were upon me, tear them out of their
semantic field day, throw out the yellow journalists
of bad grammar & terrible manner. Looks all the world
like retinal painting, mellifluous-tongued enigmatic
qualities of objects. What does that little bird symbolize?
Joseph makes mousetraps and bait boxes. Scent of
turpentine on a sweatshirt, rudeness of the dog, baby's
kindness, & a song about not being able to leave a
room. Let's have a good prank & consider it birdlike.
Rearrange the altar, reverse the position of the graven
images. It's a reflected image of you, my good man,
my good woman which is partly concealed & partly revealed.
Who's within? A man-woman made up of 5 agglomerates:
form, feeling, perception, intellect & consciousness.
It's the process of patterns of the evolution of the
world. Something is visible, something is apparent.
I am stuck in a chronology. Down on my knees with
gratitude at the Pergamon in East Berlin for how those
statues were preserved, survived a great war. The
ripples of her stony hair recalled to me the sea or
electromagnetic fields, snakes. Your eyes go mad for
a statue that comes to life. I took a trip on the Wansee
to calm down. Every thought gives off a throw of the dice
(Mallarmé). Lugubrious but also lovely, depicting the
artworks as apparatus it all comes to one: the room is
open to the public mind. Learning to behave like a coding
system, I signal you, finger to cheek, to say we must
be going, I left something breathing on the stove . . .
Is it the silver or moon condition which has to be raised
to the sun condition? No reply in this quarter of the

mistresses, the dakinis of the east. You don't have to be
inscrutable, just walk around me, observe me. I don't
have a dry mind but enter any painting with clues from
my life. This one holds a bandana, that one a mystical
hook for catching up projections. O Mode of Thought, I
make the rules. For lobby visitings sit quietly. For
hospital visitings walk swiftly through the contaminated
hallways. Have no salient entanglements with the primal
energies at this point. You are beginner's mind swimming
in the labyrinth or hope refracted through a hard glaze,
breaking into the sun condition. O man of the morn, man
of the norm, o mountain man. I would absorb the lessons
you tender, you teach, the lessons of the mathematicians
& alchemists. I finally understand that force is not
mass but also want nothing insoluble here, please. I
have an adept's unfried brain that points to one simple
thing: window dressing. Behind it? Bisexuality has
always been an act of divinity, mercury & sulphur mixing
in the chemistry of the god-goddesses. We have reached
the sky, they said, WE ARE IMMORTAL! Playing *Die Zauberflöte*
on Saturday morning makes the week converge nicely, a
delectation of the beautiful sound that would boom onto
St. Mark's Place or down the canyon from Eldora. It feels
naked to grin like creature of habit: the creature of
pinks & purples, the creature who is papa, the creature
that beats on a crate out my window says he's of Hindu
sect & causes a street argument, the Penitentes of El Rito
with their cookout & bake sale, the anonymous creatures
seeking enlightenment who live on the outer ring of
utopias, working in to the fiery center. You are on a
moving train, you look out the window & see the other
train moving. Can you now explain relativity? Creatures
that surface from the Weather Underground, creatures
that surface for you to be in love with, creature with
hair like cornsilk, creature that desires you be there
feeding, creature that draws a circle in the sand,
creature fixing a stove, taking apart a generator,
flashing the cupola with tin. Time surely doesn't go
in one direction. There is some desire to identify
oneself with conflicts related to the outside world.
Are they internal or external? This is the form part.

Imagine you are building a fortress for your ego. It
likes the padding. But it needs objects of attraction
or repulsion. It needs to make *you* substantial, you
lover, you impossible jinxed family, you money, you
Miss Preacher, you goody two-shoes. Should I go on?
Then you need to talk about these things in a language
unadorned by personality. It's so difficult. How big
is baby? He's soooooo big. Next, pleasure & pain beyond
physical sensation is the feeling part. Is that form
I see a friend or enemy? I want to reflect off you.
You make me alive, panting for more love, or else
angry about the bath episode. It is a pretense that
there is anything but me here now. The mind/body part
of feeling goes two ways. The mind part is a very
colorful fantasy of how pretty the poem could be, how
luminous that you would wonder at it. No such luck,
but the body part is my relationship to all of you, you
as solid Greg or Katie, something to count on. It is
my version of you I cling to enthusiastically, out
shopping at the Korean vegetable market. Perception is
the third agglomerate and is based on that which is mani-
fested by form and feeling and that which is not. Refer
back to ego headquarters. 25,000 miles to the ends of
the earth. Do you know about the torus, the cloud of
electrified gases circling Saturn that's 300 times hotter
than the sun? Sanskrit for something like intellect
means a tendency to accumulate a collection of mental
states as territory, mental states which are also physical.
There are 51 types of these, some associated with virtue,
some — ignorance, passion, anger, pride, doubt & dogmatism —
associated with its opposite. Then there are bold thoughts,
dogmatic beliefs (eternalism or nihilism) and the neutral
thoughts: sleep or slothfulness, intellectual speculation,
remorse & knowing. You see the point is not to condemn
one kind of thought pattern and accept another even if
it is virtuous. *All* thoughts are questionable. And
they manufacture chain reactions all the time. Like the
echo, your voice bounces back on you as well as being
transmitted to the next wall. Place two
mirrors opposite one another to get a sense of the con-
tinuity and endlessness. Infinite regress. The fifth

is consciousness, which is different from mind. Sanskrit
for *mind* literally means "heart." It's direct & simple,
requiring no brainwork. Consciousness runs behind
living thoughts, it is the kindling for the explicit
thoughts. It is the immediate available source for the
agglomerates to feed on. What we need is a gap with no
kindling twigs. The way of resolving thoughts is through
complete non-evaluation. The agglomerates won't know
what to do because their language is the language of
duality and evaluation. And that's why they keep their
thoughts in a bank! You see how it runs, develops, picks
up steam? I rehearse the speech I am about to deliver.
I notice that I had that thought before, that those wooden
saints on the cloister wall look like big gingerbread
cookies. Creature of old lumps, tender daddies, the
occasion allows a dabbling in rigor, scorn your bravura,
scatter it. Lift your arm. I lift my arm. Lift your
head. I lift my head. Book—this is book. Chair—
this is chair. Calling out to you over the Vermont night,
the New Hampshire night, the Massachusetts night, calling
out to you over the Cherry Valley night, the New York
City night, calling out to you through the California
night, through the Roman night, the Parisian night,
calling out to you over the Afghan night, calling you,
I call you, calling out to you over the Santa Fe night,
the Boulder night, calling out to you over noise of
heavy machines strapped to the boys of the block singing
out some beat I'll go out & get in step with them. I
call out to you like the angel announcing life & death
to Mother Mary & do a little dance to make myself
very small. I do this repeatedly & tell a story
something like the Merode altarpiece painting by
Campin at The Cloisters

## The Lie

Art begins with a lie
    The separation is you plus me plus what we make
        Look into lightbulb, blink, sun's in your eye

I want a rare sky
    vantage point free from misconception
        Art begins with a lie

Nothing to lose, spontaneous rise
    of reflection, paint the picture
        of a lightbulb, or eye the sun

How to fuel the world, then die
    Distance yourself from artfulness
        How? Art begins with a lie

The audience wants to cry
    when the actors are real & passionate
        Look into footlight, then feed back to eye

You fluctuate in an artful body
    You try to imitate the world's glory
        Art begins with a lie
            That's the story, sharp speck in the eye.

## Sidney's Complaynt

I think I'm in love & yet complain
Is this live, berated for not loving better?
I think I'm in love but sometimes I wonder
I want pity for being loved, yet get stone-cruel
Seeking love, love would be emptier still
Love's hot, am I burned out?
I do what's wrong to get my way beyond desire
I wail for love like I'm poor
Love me, Love me, Love me further!
Love adores itself, it's Cupid's work back & forth
or some dark goddess of perversion
who'd leave you intentionally killed by a kiss
Is it worth it to be smothered alive?
Love, Love, let me be loved, but let me complain.

## Hopes & Fears

Hope & fear hopes & fears
you have them
you had them, hopes & fears you have them

You had them, hopes
You have them, fears
hopes or fears you had them
you have them
hopes & fears you have them

I won't say no, you have them
I will say it plainly you had them
I had them, hopes & fears I have them

Wake in the morning: fear, the clock, the day, I had it
Wake in the afternoon: fear, the clock, quiet, I had it
Fear: the night, noise, the street, I have it
Person beating his body against a building, I saw it
Fear: he had it
She has it
Hopes & fears you have them
All the bodies in morning light: they have it
Wake in the morning: fear, the clock, the day, job,
another person was there, he had it
Wake in the afternoon, she was gone, he had it
Two men: one had it
Two other men: both had it, fear they have it
Two women had fear of being alone
She won't walk down the street alone or say goodbye
Then her friend needed to be talking constantly
They had it
Hopes were had by all for good weather to go apple-picking
Fear: the radio, the forecast, the debt, the man had it

Fear you might get hurt: back off, start again, go home
I have them, hopes & fears I have them
Hope to be safe, fear to be sick, injured, isolated
Hope to be in a well-heated place, a place with light,

another person in the room I want to know her
I want you: hopes & fears, I want you
I don't have you but I have hope
Fear you will quit my sight
Fear you'll no more be present in my world
I don't have you but I have fear
Fear: I have it
Do you? Do you have it?
Fear: what is it? Fear: who is it?
It isn't you it may be fear
Fear: I'm not here when I should be her
Wake in the afternoon: the clock the telephone the doorbell
Who is it?
Who are they
Are they fixing something up there?
Someone said a name, sounded like Anister Honorful
Raining on the roof: fear

I whispered her name as if to say fear
But I whispered the long way
& she said, because she was close Yes
Yes, she wouldn't have it
She won't have any of it, fear
The summer solstice a day like no other I have it
I had it then, yes
No it won't happen again, fear like that
Fear we had it
I hope to see you & then I hope to see you or
be seen by you in the room of wonderful paintings
I painted myself this way out of fear
Presentable hope in the night, I went out often
I went out hoping to see something reminding me of you

Yes, I had it and it was distinct. It was a thin hope
Someone was an outsider but I knew the name & he
shouted my name to scare me to say I know you won't be afraid
Outsider on the roof a week ago looking, he said, for a key
Are you succeeding in finding a home you look rich all right
You look rich out of fear
Hoping to be seen outside all of her attitudes

Fear to be taken apart with verbs & nouns & adjectives
Fearing to miss one event never to be repeated again
Could that be
Dare we say that
Hope he survives like the others
I read about the MX missile
It was designed to make you fierce & hopeful
but listen, are you listening      it scares us
I said it is of fear made & fear born like the
monster it is always being Everyone is saying this
over & over out of fear & hope to change the mind, the plan
the instrument of this terrible darkness
It is that simple fear again to be hope
I hope so
I certainly hope so
I meant rich in the sense of complete, not hungry
Fear eats her
We are hoping for a change in the mood
The climate is too hot for right now
I fear it isn't natural to be cooling the drinks like this
Come out from the hot sun
Fears & hopes in the little businesses
The results are promising
I had hoped to visit all the watering spots
I stopped in Brugge because I had a vision
Memling was there to paint us in our car
Was it fear?
He said we had a kind of haunted look
He wore a big Arnolfini hat but I played the bridegroom

A car is scaring the people from another century
I said it won't do not to be polite
Nothing to do with hope or fear
But I always had them both before I wrote
in this great curriculum
a prescription of hope
I watched myself grow fangs in the moonlight
I jumped back at myself
Later I turned fish to get away quick
I had them, you see of course how deceptive it is
Why have fear, why have it?

Not a lot of sense to kill the Tamil people
Sri Lanka a name you could love
The names are instruments of doom
Collectively speaking for fear for hate as in
I hate you world I kill you too
You know this
I was thinking you know this why sing about it?
Hopes & fears you have them
Hopes & fears you had them
You always had them
I won't tell you what you are
Don't tell me or don't you dare
You will be sorry to be a messenger of this
sad news if you accept this, did you ever have them?
I asked Did you do you have them, hopes & fears?
Who is metamorphosing
I want to entertain you with a rendition of something
approximately these words
Look at my eyes!
Hopes & fears, I have them
I had them
Hopes, I had them
I had fear
Hoping to cajole you into neither
I won't have it if I can't have them

Her fear is sweet to her
You sleep as this is forced on you
How can you do this
Wakening among the uncomfortable because as you see
they won't last, the root of it, fear
& hope to live forever
You are the audience of all my hopes & fears
Listen to my hopeful voice now
Inflections say this with all their might
It is in how it is being said
I told you so it was certainly not very hopeful
Fear you will shut down the amplification
before you hear about the torture of many brave
men & women
Can you imagine this?

It happens all the time
Here could be mentioned dioxin
Here is the introduction of poison
It is flourishing but will not flower
Fear: the wind will blow my topcoat off
Cambodia, can you see it?
Can you feel the fear
Hope to be out of it soon
Hope to squirm out of it
This love is one-sided, goodbye hope
She settles down & fears fear like armor
Look at our little sister fear
It was like this
Fear: the others, the school, a voice, I had it
If you have nothing you have fear
It comes out in writing
But this was prescribed to be because you had this busy
mind one day
One day it attributed itself to you
Fear likes you being mad
And fear will make you careful

But I meant to put something back
in about fear before it got so built up
You can't say that about fear she is cunning
Little Renard is afraid of the storm & hides
I watched the singers playing Dido & Aeneas
until they became sublime & went beyond
that to fear
Fear to leave, to be apart, the hero must go on to battle
An empire is forming you can't turn history around
until now
He never left & aged in her arms weak in his fear
The goddesses mock us, hope & fear
So what?
Hopes & fears we have them
Do you have it? Fear?
I suppose so
Certainly so
Yes, I have it. The day, the clock, the voice, doorbell
Cradle me in the boundary of your plan

so the limbs won't break
Break down this hope, this automatic machine
Reflex to hope
Fear in the reflection
I watched myself in the water sprout roots and blossoms
Hope to be there when the time comes
It'll just roll around you'll see
It'll just be there I tell you so
Certainly
I write this as part of the curriculum
Crank up my fears to make them go away
I see you in the rain, I see you widening
I see the big raincoat
I was waiting for you to return
Earlier I had hopes, later I had fears
Hopes & fears I have them, I had them
It went like this: the day, the equidistance, two people
went apart, a noise on the roof, I honored the dead
then a storm, I spoke on the telephone, drug addict?
A witness to lunch, the little dog hid
But it could be even more mundane: clock, money
I want to be hopeful so you get better
Fear won't heal anybody's heart
Turn it around: her fear is sweet to her
What does the congressman say
Convey her fear to him
Run for cover or stand up with the Quaker
Fear: the dogtag
My fear was her boat, her hope, and let it come out —
her ambition
It launches her it makes her wise
But let it be seen not to be such good advice
to be a victim of her whim and wonder
She would wait for fear if she had to
She would stalk fear
It is the ally of the practice of dying into life
This is strange talk
Writing is a way of canceling them out but
display the colors too
It could be pretty: fear, or fiery at least

Yes with a dress with accouterments
I like the panic that hangs about the window
St. Mark's Place
His sex because he was older (she was a child)
scared her, fear of something you've never seen before
But another one said this never scared her
so she was always secure
Fear you will bite my head off
How I wished to see her face but that was the one part
she would not reveal
He has big paranoid ears
What are they saying about me
A pointed demon, a table of jumping objects, moonless time,
someone calls you out of sleep
Dream my mother was ferrying me to the afterlife in
a gondola through a subway tunnel
Fear I would fall over into the murky depths, underbelly New York
Fear: never see light
Fear: all my hair is chopped off, you don't recognize me
Fear: laughter from the mouths & bellies of vicious animals
Phantoms of a skittish head
I was created in a test tube
The train halted in the middle of Bulgaria, rude officials
demanded papers in an obscure language and took money
Fearful of prison: Iran
They exit with your passports behind curtains, doors, partitions
Cold eyes
My hope goads me on to further raptures
to win the sestina contest!
Let them come to some agreement, everyone suffers
Wake at night: someone going through the bags
Wake at dawn: perfunctory cold & hunger
Old bogeyman Totalitarianism
Fear: life under the gun
Hopes & fears hopes & fears you have them
you had them you have them still
Hopes & fears you have them
Hope to see all the spectacles
Fear I misplaced them
Fear I missed them

jockeying for favor with one more powerful
Traveling by airplane I had them
Traveling in the blue sky I had them
All the precautions make you have them
You are the audience of all my hopes & fears.

## It Sounds It

1
You & I out of all dreaming:

Of this you are understood, of measurement, of predicament.
I fear I do not exist we'll not exist you give a candidate
such a time, predicated on false belief. Over a small town's
cab radio: Pick up Stevie Wonder at Harvest House. Not a
blink or raised lash but static of reserve. Now pick up
Eldridge Cleaver who is "passionately against Welfare."
Make a remark: Time, how strange you are to us. Make your
mark, the European would say, free of the wild weed of delusion.
We are all after all all of us as often as not on the mark.
On the money. Freeze these assets and markedly lethal weapons.
Of course you may curse what has been done to you Dear Member
of the Senate. Dear Warrior Woman of Blatant Dimension: the
space inside equals theoretic bedtime story. She is a princess,
of course, that some flesh-tone touch-tone Princess, the same
American stammerings calling after a Yellow Cab. If I ask
for a pen he thinks I'm going to a fare check or check this
wondering myself at many things, dollars. Of course not a
whole city went & sealed this occasion in anyone's favor
at a primary in any cabbie's mirror. Lauper at U. of C., Jackson
in Denver & all the daughters went & sealed this occasion.
The seal & mark of any fair time is what you're doing, what
I'm in any moment renouncing any influence from him, her,
it, them in medias res, restless & absorbed all about moving,
to move or be moved went the time the tide went the good
nature went as mute as any comment or seal with a western
kiss. He's taken the measure in a prodigious glare, something
said much greater than it sounds . . .

A slow mind served the candidate well, the mark of any animal
petted down, below the chair. Ah, the dog can't vote.
I mark the ballot like a good citizen. I can make a cross
like anyone ought to be able to but is it a delusive LAST DAY
to register October 5th? Went the Harvest time, all fall
down. Did Wonder vote? Will Cindy bop or Black Elk speak?
Moved west, went the theocratic resolve using language to say

something that's never been said: like: What is mirrored in
language I can't use. But agreeing nonetheless with she, I,
they, the consolation nearest her with genius in his eye (not
the senator) but a scenario: She had a female lover they got
married & got her brother to donate sperm so she, the other,
could have the baby but then they broke up & she wants
Visiting Rights, her brother's child, she's nothing but a
doting aunt. But what would the Platform say to this? Is
it perverse in Dorn's sense as "against the family?" I'm
waiting on a great moment, pulling the lever all welcome all
the new citizens who always glide off with smoothness to
another subject. The political nightmare the mark of the
lesbian, the concomitant, the looser ones, coming unhinged
in an impious way, like the student who falls off his chair
when I read Olson aloud, he flaps wings, his arms are a
wheel or whorl, where are we going in anyone's lurid imagination?
Names who are the repository for anybody to touch. You
touch me, touch me, don't bristle. The cat assaults the
image, a virtuous act to be not so expectant, as a child
says "exposed to," he's supposed to not never know nothing
better. An authoritarian voice provides all the
corrections wanting to rip the "reals" out of their mouths:
real good, real nice, real smart, real never speaking to me,
real silence, real prompt, real enough of what I know, real
strong, real quick lift to the issue, backbone, femur. To
say all that before counting on me: real pressure, real death.
real everything almost with the smile of a child, real
Nicaragua, no slate can hold the figures as he makes them
stand at attention, tiny soldiers & villains in space. The
space is my villain, he says, rocked back into bed, & you
are my only mother: real sky, real scarce, how long do you
give me, real obvious ploy, real temperament, real terror,
real turf, clean-cut walkways, real sweet, real animals,
genuine food.

I'll stand again as if in trance under Jupiter for the passage
of middle years, witness the cast of any vote. Like the priest
Mayans they would pick a low energy day, no full or beginning
moon, no ground swell, a waning situation so the activists
stay home. Come out of your delicate rooms into the discreet
booths of fixed chance. A ruse or result, a resumed situation,

a sense of subtle wantonness, what is at stake. Irritation,
damnation, poverty, cruelty, neglect, real easy, but if I
thought what you thought or if whoever you are thought whatever
she could never figure out, or if they all went, acknowledged,
acclaimed the Tibetan doctor's advice to one young son that
he not watch scary movies or moves, the . . . Eyes move over the
intensely white linen, the semigloss off-white walls, a
rattan sofa, the newly waxed floor, the front door with a
Christian symbol marked in metal, a, emblem, a, place, an,
incision, a, how in the world you've done it, a world, or
how in the world your vitals scared at your own heroism an
act of violence. A signet, a peace treaty, the depiction of
a Buddhist deity with eyes in her hands, feet. Eyes everywhere,
totally awake.

# WAKE UP

Every single proposition can be brought to a particular form
in this case a wild shout

# MAKE IT UP

You the proxy, you the volunteer
or cast a  VOTE, A SHADOW, A FIRST STONE

as a signal to begin counting. The loser concedes winning
is the order of the day, a command, the eyes shut down real
fast predicting rain

Also, there was a bay horse for me to ride, as in my vision


2
Begun to throb, their human questions
comparison with other life forms:
urgent to communicate with his lips
become more interesting or what has kept you?
a jewel brilliant & hard
what has kept you
a tree with a bird in it, a holiday
what has kept you

a nightmare, a frightening cleaver
what has kept you
a book making sense, a robber in the street,
one gooseneck lamp
what has kept you
an illogical situation, a job to do
my own lassitude, am I late?
Am I to punctuate this mark
like a small prayer
forever  supining
supplicating
forever obscuring, like a tall Sally
like a long tall Sally, like Sally's ride
what comes  next?
So I won't play you that trick
In a long tall column
I won't put my mark here
what did I do
I'm all shook up, garbled a sentence
lost the small battery
found  the  neighborhood
changed, what did I do?
scarce knew  what:
run, walk, speak, wonder
speak, sing, vo-code
every last syllable
her expression had of being most natural
eyes fixed as of a mute statue
heart of bronze
what  happened?
a wedding, a death, one small story
the death of a small store
what  happens?
A tremendous bristling explosion
the air of that amplitude is now doubtless strange
It sounds strange to me
It sounds like stepping back into a room
where I wasn't ready to go out there yet

MX Trident Minuteman Poseidon
too thick for going out there yet

not a matter in dispute
what happened?
but a stockpiling
what happens?
the leaders speak as if under water
mesmerized by a mythical deterrent
abhorrent detergent
what? What happens?
we look for the detriment or a measure
of the possible wretchedness
You are not a space treaty in my dream
but villains in space

I, I, and I, & yet again I
& you are you are you are you yet again
you
out of all dreaming

I or I or I or you but you but you
out of all dreaming

I say what you think or think I say what
you think
do I?
You think I'm thinking like you
am I?
you think you can say it?
Can we agree on any of the issues?

in the light, I am not at all dreaming
in the light of this predicament
blatant dimensions, the situation continues
out of hand

hand it over
or handle with care
welfare

A man of public office
entered the party for the Nicaraguan delegates
at whose instigation?

with a cane
Cyclops?
Spiderman?
Hidden behind brute eyes
invoke a terrible time
of espionage
Return to a vatic voice
O help us Medicine Buddha
"grassroots" inroads
Jalapa, your torn spirit
bounces back
in the fortitude
of one Selfida Hernandez
Her gaze is steady:
what eyes have seen
where she's been
Torture
out of all dreaming
the old game:
who's doing it to whom
murder at the Honduras border
she & her dead son out of all dreaming
muscles out of all being
this weakened white person
sits at the top of the food chain
write or try to witness
try to get behind her eyes *en español*

*por favor*

*mi amiga*
*esperanza*

Understood back of human questions
a throb
murmur of the huge collective life
putting forth not exactly perfections
as the candidate rouses a smile
musters the old geography
looks haggard
but comes to life on any issue

would renunciation provide a moral glamor?
give up the inbred suspicion
hand o'er the privy purse
a long career behind him,
ardently over the finished meal
the ruse, the counterintelligence
the samurai in me wants to engage
your attention for a long time
as long as it takes
to win the man
the moral fiber
behind the eyes
rods & cones in my
preternatural laboratory of stimulation
not losing game or battle
it sounds like the first part of
a symphony

announce my theme & come on in
make the place your own
it sounds
it comes to me
The creation story told by Tibetan doctor
how semen mixed with moisture on a leaf
it made a woman outta me
she bops & all the daughters went & sealed this occasion
& the goddess of poetry Sarasvati shook her body
& strummed her vina
the plants stopped fussing
any hairdo you want for sale on any mall
her locks coiled in spirals of sound
nothing costs dollars
in the light of
acute & deliberate action
I mean you can't get anything done for that
at the Target store
I was aiming to get there
on a blind date

3
Newton showed that for every action there
is an equal & opposite reaction. This
holds true for the arms race as it does
in physics

"Anything you undertake is based on outlook"

a 17-year-old friend's
point of
character
is on a line
how to be
a good one
want
the world
to think
well
of him

I remember, too,
lying to save my grace

little Lego towers
the 4 directions
& arms like ram's horns
remind me of
upheavals
on a Zapotec rug
accidents in the wool

clear sentences he said he wanted
blasting Carla

it sounds like my last mistress
it sounds like my mistress's eyebrow
it sounds like a 25-gallon acid spill

Syntax technicians rushed to the scene, fire personnel
put a temporary seal on the ruptured fitting, & soda ash
on the spill to neutralize the hydrochloric acid
Vulcan spokespersons could not be reached for comment

What you say is what you are
You might be a naked booby star

It sounds like what you meant to be saying

It sounds like they memorized their debate
You were saying something?
It sounds all wasted & thou has hands
thou hast ears thou shalt die of a thousand thous
It sounds, & yet to be understood

It sounded like a good idea

It sounds of darkness, day gone
An ancient scar upon this picture
It sounds like much to this man or woman is due
It sounds: my heart doth bind
It sounds not a lot like stagecraft

Words remain in memory
their essential simplicity & strength
like open air & fresh water elements

He hath learned a trick from Flavio
It sounds hot on the tongue but later
it's cool, or rather it sounds cold
A creature remains in the room
although you know
I don't think we were created at all
as well as try to find out any's thoughts
& tread the sun & be more bright than he
I thought it sounded a bit obscure
keep the obsequies in mind, the decline
of a noble ignoble arms race


4
Where does it gather
or gathered it not here, potable & compendious

Of this you aren't stood for or stood up to because you are
the president. Do you know him the child asks and what
is he? is he a man? a voice? a radio? what is it or rather
no one would ever want to do that in another dimension like

175

Teddy Roosevelt. Would you? Would Groucho Marx? So much
faith on either part but knowing the facts or having depth
or dice. No dice but it could represent a lost ballot.
No mercy will burn the coals, stroking the pleasure of
poetry with the pleasure of politics or of other puzzles,
you name any kind of respite needed here:

HELP

Jeane Kirkpatrick says we all knew Brutus was an honorable
man whose poems passed from hand to mouth in manuscript
before the onslaught of these waves

it sounds like rubbish to me
or irresponsible, meaning the same
it sounds pugilistic & strange
"to the stars through difficulties"
or something like that
something said that was supposed to be
naming your own fate, to say it slant
slant-out,  politician-like
What are you driving at?
You, out of all dreaming
but to those of us who unkindly were
scattering to shine it makes no sense

Petty thoughts go off
it sounds rather like a wonderful place
to go off to but
it sounds fishy
the people are bewildered
the people are inebriated
by the magnificence of the scene

To be a little wilderness
Who would guess?
to be so coy
or compare a great thing with a small one

& out of all dreaming,

this  scheme

## Crack in the World

I see the crack in the world

My body thinks it, sees the gaping crack in the world

My body does it for me to see

Blood flowing through the body crack

Body, send your rivers to the moon

Body twists me to the source of the moon

It turns me under a wave

It sets up the structure to make a baby, then tears
it down again

Architecture of womb-body haunting me

Someone is always watching the ancient flow

It doubles up my mind

Ovum not fertilized

I see the crack in the world

Thoughts intersect in the body

He must not keep me down

Let me go my way alone tonight

No man to touch me

A slash in me, I see the slash in the world tonight

It keeps me whole, but divides me now

Out on land, to bleed

Out on street, to bleed

In the snow, blood

This is a South American song

Scent of oleander

Or this is a cactus song

Sing of a blood flower a rose in the crotch

O collapsible legs!

My body enchanted me to this

My body demented to this

It is endometrium shedding

I am compressed in the pressure of my heart

It is life pursuing the crack in the world

Between worlds

Between thoughts

A vacant breath

Words won't do it

Ovum not fertilized

The man hasn't done it

I cover every contingency
the catty one
or puritan walking in a fecund world

Words sing to me of endometrium collapse

Words go down to my belly

Back swelling, to put my body next to the earth

This is periodic

It comes at the full moon

Let me go howling in the night

No man to touch me

Don't fathom my heart tonight, man

No one wants to be around this factory,
this beautiful machine
but I shun your company anyway

My flexible body imagines the crack

Body with winds

See the crack in the universe

The curse, glorious curse is upon me

Don't come to my house

Don't expect me at your door

I'm in my celibacy rags

My anthropocentric heart says there's
a crack in the world tonight

It's a long woman's body

It's a break in the cycle of birth & death

It's the rapid proliferation of cells
building up to die

I make up the world & kill it again & again

I offer my entrails to the moon

Ovum not fertilized

Architecture haunting me

Collapsible legs you must carry the world

You get away from me

You keep your distance

I will overpower you with my scent
of life & death

You who came through the crack in my world

You men who came out of me, back off

Words come out of the belly

Groaning as the world is pulled apart

Body enchanted to this

Body elaborated on this

Body took the measure of the woman
to explain the fierceness of this time
walking on the periphery of the world.

## Triolet

A perfectly clear liquid like water
flows out of the spine

Last night in the hospital, this is what I saw

I don't know where this fluid sits
& what its design

A perfectly clear liquid like water
flows from her spine

Does it move from the brain in a line?

The cool doctor draws it out with a straw

A perfectly clear liquid like water
flows out of the spine

Last night, in the cold hospital, this is what I saw.

# HELPING THE DREAMER

*"some kind of transmission, Aw cut it out"*

## Coup de Grace

You say you know what's up, what's what, what is or isn't true, what's a modicum or midge of delight. A small very small being. Well you'd need beauty to go with the truth part hand in hand or hand over head or head over heels in love with him. You'd need it, sure. And sure a trace, sure a quarry is the heart. Excavation. Open season. To open the season here and nourish the surer part. Immiscible friends. Inadmissible facts to find a cure place a safe place to live with great store for feeding, great schools, outlets of all kinds for every pudendum, nail, blind, drain, towel rack, bulb, spring, washer, plug. Not to be a piker about shopping but all the time wanted the glorious objects to glow you with their radium dials not enough to make you ill. You want to see the chemistries, the tiny tit-magics of the chemical-alchemical world, of the astronomical-astrological world. You want to see the elements in their element. Element of style or styles, all shading leaving a blend to be 100 percent cotton, 100 percent wool, 100 percent milk. Confront their faces, their peculiar labels, their ruthenium. It is rueful or ruthless? How can the family make a gesture to the sidewalk we would all understand? Would it be daughter to mother, father to daughter, son to mother, sister to brother? The family needs caulking, the family needs oakum, the family is in a continual flux of birth, old age, sickness, death & ducking. Caprioles? Can a horse take responsibility? Can it rake, does it dance? Sure, a sheen of her aura dispels the gloom, sure you keep brushing your hair and the world shines. The novitiates are all of them in a soup. Soup de grace. Are you spilling over into the darker part because when you see a so-called socialled enemy you duck into a convenient hammerlock. Take my arm, you'll need a plea on this one, this oddity of concrete, lumber and confusion, or this oddity of kernel, hackle & callboards. Can you be torn apart, does it betoken a separation, does the taskmaster care you're all of a piece, does it make a pretty pie or pretty schedule? You say you can see a brilliant new adventure coming and would pack your navigational instruments. Canst thou by searching define the universe? You might try to define the distance but it may be a mistake to divide the people into sharp groups & in a turnabout the distance stalks you. Build up my desire. Make it of pongee & hansom, take me as reality opposed to experience, then toss it off, an old skin, an old rug, a throwaway, discarding the clutter of the known world, gold cufflinks of Anwar Sadat. The clutter you would tell of, would get you down, being unseen, being of a letterhead nature, so personal, necessary and underneath flowers: stars, nativities, Underneath any refuse is what you make of it. Hidden? Under the rug. Or standing in a gown, from *gunna*, medieval Latin for loose robe or fur. I'm gonna wrap it up. Can you eke out a smile. Are you stingy in your appreciation of our numinous galaxy, our circle of poets, artists, dancers. Not a lot of dissonance from the audience, please not a lot of duty either nor let it be known this is forced on them by dint of some way things got put together, things got done. You say you heard what's going on in a surefire way. You take your radishy gossip to the bevy collective. And at this juncture be it known you are aiding and abetting or fading and regretting the time the two met, or one walked away coolly from that other one. And smiled. And slept. And went on powdery and strange, alien for the likes of us, clairvoyant and all. Is it only a sneer that commands you masquerade this Halloween in the gait of something maternal? Leonine. Using escape velocity to do myself out of it rather than make a fuss about trying to get together. Roseate sky it behooves you to speak of in your wanderings, your questionable affairs of the heart, your tabletops, jovial home belongings in the sense that you belong there too. You. Or you beside some proud reviewing stand, a small Anarchist hidden inside trying to get out. Or the occasion of your wrath was something caricatured in a scramble for choice cuts. Admonition newly turbaned, a howl of philistines being apprehended my brightest diamond, my jewel, apprehended at the fin de siècle, forever drinking *fine* with two sets of eyebrows, one painted above the other. But now it is a delight to remember sonorously, not imitate with a hint of icy mockery your withering sarcasm, your beer garden in Berlin. I am appearing in you landlocked, by forceps and barely breathing to enter the world. Harsh to be a bearer of misfortune, turned around so that now they wear the leotards of the highwire, the golden panties and tops, a bright spectacle. The habit of struggle against odds, darling, harsh to be alone in political spectrum to be called at from the depths of a puddle openmouthed. Harsh to be of acidity made dwelling in a city of bores and maniacs and forever talking about money. Harsh light, harsh street, harsh in a clique of hero-heroine worship for the dull epoch we live. You leave here, see how long it stretches, gets you. You robbing your youth of its prerogative: travel. And harsh in your rosy view of pornography, impatient you might say a brutal society of earning powers. You harsh among the nightwalkers of 3rd Avenue. The worker maybe has a motherland, a tribute to authority which exercises a spell. She has discussions with herself. She preserves her notoriety, no matter fanaticism, no matter the fickle and valiant witnesses. Fickle because they mock it in the first place, valiant because they still emerge from woodwork like nerve-storms. The soul of harness lives in the floodgates, appears on the ramparts with the rest of history, that horizon of gleaming lozenges. You say you know the delights. And all that sparring with partners of opposite sizes, with partners the size of a small being. You say you know. Know too how we are yearning to love each other.

If we could, would it be advisable, would it be wise? Wise to bring in household pandemonium after all the monarchy. Because you do love to see a sofa set right, and all the party things laid out invitingly. I won't be criticized for my napkins nor the trouble I take to bake something abnormal, not betrayal but loyalty to the ongoing quality of life. Avert disaster, don't dish out the final blow, let's die into each other. To have spake such faith out loud is the poetry part, the part that wants reading to be done to enter my experience. And this is the personal part too, in love with liberty, not confiscated for a song. Civilized is the word to come to mind. Why they know nothing of it (or seem to care to) but what's doled out by the reigning loudmouths. Preying on my sympathy with a symphony. The tinkling of Clytemnestra's bracelets is heard in the percussion, counting on the receptivity of present-day ears. Listen to me going on this way like a babbler, like the tendency my astrological sign is prone to, like a stonewaller, like a grievance, like a woman streaked with grey, magnificent in cape and soft felt hat, like a

184

toilet article, like the critics' scorn, like humorous oratory. Oratorical, a penetrating vision of the world, wouldn't you say, would you stand up, say it loud and clear? And vivid are the agitation machines trying to get at the heart of it, my speech. But you are hired to clear the hecklers, transmute their desire and occurrences. For they are but the reflection of a smoking weapon that went off once long ago, and is only ghost reminder not to kill. She said she couldn't understand, being newly hired, the way the customers spoke the menu items in French, & begged our indulgence. It sounds like some kind of delicious item, *coup de grace*, of mercy & deliverance.

And deliver me up to your fine humming, deliver me in the morning to the first bird, let them go on fighting, I won't be had for a tag. You need leaf beauty to go indisputably along with your tragic theme, or comic & lighthearted as the case may be, but when I see so much dying around me, then how much of it, going on without someone, may I absorb? For they leave an impression where the body was. And you put your hand in to have a blessing and it is a grasping shadow. And you are there to size shadow up, always saying you were an accident, an ancient bystander, never taking an active role, but a more alluring one. I wanted no part of the open season but it descended with the weather before I could hold out my hand, say no. But yes the greatest iniquities are resounding in my heart. Am I alone in my fustiness my diversion my love of narration, the wanting to end epigrammatically? Or axiomatically. Or winningly. You know about common sense, how it grows on you, and the pier glass. And the pillowcase. And the soundboard. And the trousers. And the burnt brunt of this worldly confusion because although I live overproportionedly and lavishly I do so with a mind, overeager and overlapping with yours. For you are but the gracile part of a larger *mal du pays*. And we all weep for home at birth, a strident cry which is not to say of womb made. I won't dollop up more platitudes but make some gesture to release the harsh animal in your setup. A shaking of this left arm and my wild-faced expression should banish it away. Tell me, friend, if dollar diplomacy is working in those faraway places. Do you shy away from the frequent hostage taking. It is dangerous? Canst be thyself and true?

185

## Artemis

I pray you are always above me
Imperial Ruler of the Stars
with your silver new-moon-bow,
arrows swift as science

You strike trees dead
fell a wild hind
& finally a city of unjust men
(I dreamt last night of warring Jerusalem)

Chaste sprite, spicy nymph,
wounding witch, any guise you wish
No hesitation, Dakini of Incantation
Command your spike deep in my heart

So I may ride, hunt, speak, shine
midwife your sting.

# Ancient Song Rising

Salute Gravettian-Aurignacian
    Venus figures which are in themselves
        The colors of a neolithic morning

Pale as skin, as desert, the makeup you neglect
    While the conquerors arrive & startle the ladies
        Just come from chat, sitting in acacia's shade

Trying out suitable made names:
    Lioness of the Second Assembly, Ubiquitous Holiness,
        Lady of High Places, Primordial Child-to-a-Star,

Girl of a busy Monday through Friday, Charm Boatess,
    Explorer Who-Clears-Her-Throat-Dramatically,
        Anatomist Morning, fiery Agni, Au Set

Which sets these gals off, ready for battle
    Tossing their eyebrows to the winds,
        Shedding sentimental dreams puddled with oceans

With sundown, with crazed mutterings
    Ash on thermal currents flicking
        The keening woman of an old measured stride

Tucking Patriarchal memory behind the ears
    Throw off sorrow, a random syncopation
        Let it fall apart like wounded raiments, no tears

The refrain swells: No more, no more tears!
    Then stretches to the edge of the ignoble lexicon
        Where words collide out of igneous rubble.

## Mother's Curse

*for Diane di Prima*

Out of my pen: curses ride down
Out of sky: appearance
Out of space: apparel
A bolt of insight, a cloth, tapestry
It rolls down
You rise up to meet it, your eyes alive
And it rises up within you
And it comes down, curses ride down
You meet the faces of women who look like rocks,
    who glitter like rocks
Who were fixed in stone
Who were beaten by the weather
Who have been outside for millions of years
Girls' faces too, the sister of someone Dutch
And someone who painted milkmaids knew the faces I'm
    seeing here
And someone who traveled to a darker continent knew
    the faces I'm seeing here
Eyes ride down, eyes glitter like jewels
Bright teeth of the tiger in the dark faces
    I'm seeing here
Arms adorned with intricate designs I'm seeing here
Patterns carved on faces to exaggerate the waves of electricity
    I'm seeing here
Lips moist & hungry
Bodies fly, you might say, like witches
I've seen them bolting
They are always in motion
They won't sit still
Eyes move & freeze in more than a hundred poses
Gestures for every finger & wrist & palm & arm
Rainbow fingers drum the air (I see them here)
Red beckons in seduction, blue points, is cool
Green motions you to hurry, yellow is plump & ringed
    with diamonds, all fingers strum the air
They roar all the notes of cursing,

188

Give birth to emptiness again & again
They arrive to show you chaos
They ride down, curses ride down
Strike any pose, they'll trip you up
These women of more than a thousand poses do that
I had that doubt that arises before I strike any pose
This one has you lying down, arm over eyes to hide
    from light
Or that one had you spread for sex
I had that doubt that I could ever really sleep
Or I had that doubt about love
I doubt I thought more about it than that doubt
Hesitation as in What next?
As in Next, please
What happens? The same doubt
Doubt like that, that one-pointed doubt
Curses ride down
I doubted the way the doubt seemed to me self-seeking
And then I doubted the mind that thinks that
I was afraid of dying
I was afraid of her dying
The mind that thinks I was afraid of dying I doubted
That thought took the panic of dying
& turned back on itself
Curses ride down, a band of women to haunt you
& turn everything back on itself, back on myself
A mother's curse
Not to be able to give birth this place, this time
It comes around barren this time
A mother's curse to launch on you
You who doubt
You who are settled in your territories
Who hold the absolute power-strands
You who wish to inflict more suffering
Who glut your bellies on the suffering of others
Who swallow and chew up the existence of others
Who snuff out a small body's flame
Who spit out the stuff of others
It comes around barren this time
Mother: hysteria
Mother: I loved the way you went about testing me

Mother: the lights are on me now
I can't do what I planned
It surges back on me all I did
To get this way to be in this moment now it comes back
        on me all I plotted
All I desired to accomplish without you
Mother: hysteria in the mountains
Mother: hysteria on the plains
Not settled in the territories
Chaos on the ground
These curses ride down
You ride up to meet them, eyes alive
O Mother lust I suck your nipples
I suck the dugs of the monkey & the dog
Milk turns to blood
Tears turn to blood
Flesh turns to stone
Barren this time
You grow hard under me mother
You push me off your belly
I thought you were soft
You rip the nipple from my mouth
I am tested by your fierce winds
I wanted to climb on top of your warm body
        but you withered before my eyes
Your lips turned wooden
Your tongue hid from me
Your sharp teeth pierced my skin
I am happy I arouse you
Don't destroy me
Your breath like a tempest parts me from you
You gave me birth, & parted from me
You cursed me
I was too busy in the day, & played by night
Curses come down
I'm seeing them now ride down like angels
I'm seeing them ride down now like harpies
No hiding place down here
You followed me, no hiding place down here
I met the faces of women who resembled the doubts I had
They were like you, no hiding place
You left me hanging
190

You wore out my desire
You tempted me always to manifest my desire &
        finally it wore out
Everywhere I turned I saw you
Everywhere I turned I met you
As I faced the mountain: mother's curse
Take back all you said, you said
As I faced the ocean, it came toward me
O take back all I said, it said
The ocean was my androgynous mother
        who cursed me, lured me, spat me back out
O take back all I say!
As I crawled, belly to the hot sands, thirsty, I cried
        Take back all I say
I remembered all I said and I said Take it back   invoked a mother's
I invoked a mother's revenge
        for being barren this time
Take back all I said, all I say
Abort this moment
O take back all they said
They lied about treaties, about poisoning
        the fish and the fowl
There is no sleep no peace in the money-realm
They swoop down, they come down now
With a thousand angry faces
Their faces contort to make you remember the
        ineptitude of that last moment
That was the moment you lied
You cheated in that last moment to salvage your doubt
O take back all you say
Never to be trusted, take them back
Mouths of the women become holes in the sky
        as they suck in and spit out all you say
It propagates the chaos
How will you ever get born this time?
Your doubt will be born in this chaos
The moment will work against you
O take back all I say
May these things never happen and may
        they always happen, curses ride down
A thousand women fill your room

You are crushed as they press upon you like stone this time
They trample you with their many red legs
Their bodies will always emanate the color of your desire
O wear it out, the curses ride down
Abort the moment you had that doubt about the song you sang
Freeze the gap before you spoke ill to him
She let you go on, why?
You invoked the curses that ride down
        as you let yourself be witnessed, gazing in the mirror
Holding this moment so you could own him
You tore him up to own him
You put the objects in the house to own them
They infiltrated the room to crush you, to take them back
To smash all your attachments to what you owned
They took back the territories & showed you your lies
They cursed all murderous intent as they tore you apart
O take back all I say
Too late? Freeze the moment before I say what I say
Revoke all ill
Nothing you plan will ever happen when you are in a mind
        like this
You will live in the shade
The street you live on is named Thwarted Desire
Your licenses and all credit will be revoked
Nothing you plan will be made to happen
You will be slowed
Speech will be useless here
Don't bother to articulate
Take it all back
You thought this thing, this great doubt, was supposed
        to happen
It could have happened
It will never happen
It was ready to happen
It promised to be something you could collect and take
        with you
It was willing to happen as you prepared the ground
But you were hasty
You were forcing the words and the people around you to respond
Your guts spilled out & you were not to have this happen
        ever even once in this life

A book spoke things to you
A man spoke things to you
You were invited to dance
The music spoke to you
The music cornered you with its beauty where suddenly there
    was a gap & the piano came in
You stopped
You could never be that fine
The liquid quality of the sound threatened you
You couldn't hear it except through your own demented ears
Your feet wouldn't move
The floor held you fast
You were held by your fantasy of this floor
Your arms flailed about clawing the air
You dropped to your knees
You waited too long
You had had the wrong idea to come here
You had followed the scent of your passion
It had dissolved even as you arrived
The room was a trap
Take it all back!
I say it again: take it back
Out of my pen: wind
Out of my pain: this song
Curses ride down, these women with their stretched bodies,
    their masses of hair, and nails like claws
They remind you of your doubt and desire
They laugh as they guard you against yourself
That seed won't ripen when you plant it like that
The clouds didn't materialize
The baby wouldn't grow
Wind died down
You were barren one more time
You kept waiting
What you awaited had already occurred
The obstacles held you fast
Your hands were manacled all night
You were hounded for what you owed
When the machines broke down you couldn't move
You wrote down this moment as you caught it, curses come down,
    riding toward you

You expanded the moment to include all stymied desire
Your doubt which came at the moment you noticed yourself
    thinking was the link to desire
They came down, curses ride down, to stop you
To throw the fixed switch off they come
To trample on your exaggerated corpse
To interfere with the doubt that kept you hidden
Out of the sky: voices to tease you
Out of space: they materialize to taunt your false desire
In every woman's face: dissembling
In her eye: the play of light & shadow
In her gait: the beginning and end of childhood
In her ear: the ancient cavern
Her rainbow body comes down to color your desire
She stops you in your tracks
She entwines herself around your body
Her hues reflect your willingness to glow
Glow as you stop in your false desire
Gather up your force of Take it back, take it all back
    to hurl your mother's curse against the wind here
To hurl a mother's curse we summon power from the moment
    before doubting and taking the wrong turn
We go into the gap & recharge here
Curses to the Western lands for strutting their riches, their
    arrogant way of going about maintaining a craving for more
When I had that thought about the WestI too am stuck in it
Take back my riches, take back what I say
Curses to the Eastern lands, what is the tribal mind there?
Why so much bloodshed? The warlords keep coming
And to the North I hurl this warning: the glacier is melting
& curses to the tyrants of the South, let the people go
Who am I ranting in a confused mind, in the chaos of the
    moment after I missed the point
O take back all I said
A cloth was the beginning of the appearance of how those
    women came down, curses hurtled at the planet
I rose up to meet them, eyes alive
To meet the faces of women who take the words out of my mind.

## Helping the Dreamer

It seems you've been misled through
the wrong instrument which would have you
wind tears around trees, would have you
devote your head to biology, the history
and cost of reproduction in *Daphnia pulex*,
would have you gibbering of night things
glassy water of the bay, unmitigated blackness,
sleek fur, a sharp hoot, butane lamps

The air full of music now, those runnels
speak to me, human and mechanical images
meshed together, speak to me gliding
around a room crosshatched with your desire,
speak in low smoke tones, monosyllabic,
dry, the repeated pattern of flowers
on wallpaper, speak a language I'll
understand (smiling lips and eyes)

Speak to master your shuddering, and
the surface looks you in the eye
which is how it seems, some kind of
ecstasy instead of taut anger which
dissolves into the indelible feeling that
you've always lived to be in this moment
stretched out between serenity and turmoil
this world you pounce on with your heart

Which has been loitering and hidden
in the havoc of the same instrument which
operates like an anemone in the first
touch of an idea, say, that you live
in a lair of fear and quick-panting
That your body could be mentally prepared
for any ride, that life is a maze-room,
the busy clicking of a computer, that

It's all over your head, petulant and sombre,
That it rides you, the dreamer, bitterly
disappointed in the weather, in the
gawky shapes of friends who haunt you,
biorhythms in a tangle, refusing to be
relegated to anyone's pocket, returning
the jeers, your footsteps quicken to get you
out of here, out of your brute nature

A difficult technique, stuff in the blood
stream, coursing to seep its aureole
into the sky in front of you, the sky a
forehead of the fathers, a large reflection
of whoever they may be in any mythical sense
while you are set up as Mother Earth
The colors conspire to make you glow and
your crepe-soled boots set up a reverberating

Echo though the landscape which is only
your projection anyway, newborn mountains
steaming from the sea, old-born negotiations
of civilizations about who can and can't reside here
Here with your white skin, your tinny voice,
telepathic gifts, inspired by the climb in
horror and astonishment, seeing how everything
works and co-exists, laboratories of

Discretion and secrecy, true believers
in shadow-power, believing in the solidity
of gadgets that do the appointed jobs,
axis of belief structures falling apart
accepting caprice as natural door into
the unknown, and slithering back inside
to the heart which would now like to
relax in soft upholstery, a contradictory parallel

To life as you experience it out here
on the wild hill. Hold back and let the
clothes speak, tight at groin, let the
buildings you left below speak of their
being so square at edges, let the
architects speak of their maniacal designs
to control and imprison space, making it
lucrative in a false version of comfort

Let more places open up with the names of
initials. B.C.'s, J.R.'s, J.J.'s, M.O.'s
as if it's hip to be in shorthand and
"cute" while out on the pond the shifting
ice groans its name of mutability and promise
The geese are also handsome in the light
honking their presence out of sorts or in tandem
while I'm sorting the crumpled papers

which speak of worshiping Ninni-zaza
Akkadian goddess whose eyes were clouded
by love, who was replaced by Saint Simeon
centuries later and then the world gets
married again to yet again another male saint, how
if these words could be hammered back by
an alien planet, what would we make of them?
What are the dimmest memories of solar systems?

Anomalies of man and woman power, as the new/old
comet appears in the sky in the region
of Jupiter before the watchful eye of the
perpetual "watcher" who remains arrogant
till he blisters under the hot sun and is
left to comment on all this as some kind of
irritable miraculous mistake, not being able
to understand that the plateau ahead

would be just right for getting
around with relatives, anyone who has ever
been part of you, next to you, that it *is* hospitable
this great warm earth, that it's all here:
the stormy sky, the fragrant trees, the
tenacious lichen, while elsewhere a woman
in all artifice dyes her hair black underneath
to convey secret mourning for a lost lover

Both, both. Both the way you want it,
and the way it is. Both staying and leaving.
Both memory and no memory, both things that
can tell lies and things that don't know how,
both acquiescing and resisting, both familiar
and strange. Both sheer and thick, both
separated and together, walking and standing still
Both audible and silent, both flat and round

And you are never not linked up with how
you perceive it all and how it really is,
all the messages of the sublunary sphere
at a time fueled by the iron fist of profit-
and-gain, what makes it all run, a time
which seems to be smiling nonetheless
as if to say perhaps the moon's in the
wrong corner of the sky, look up and see

## The Stick

Crumpled paper, little stick
brandished by a boy. The boy sings:
"My heart is a lion cub's!"
He is the light of my day
He primps to be a magical beast.

His mother cries "Silly beast,
little friend with stick legs
Come rouse the pretty day
You know how to sing the ditty
'My heart is Mamma's jewel'"

"Of course, Mamma, I'll clamp your
heart too. I am woman-hater beast
who want only to rip at your titties
And pummel your butt with a stick
I want to chase you through the day"

The mother wants to forget the day
The boy came of age with all his heart
It was a stick beating her heart
She'd been supplanted by a beast
who would seduce the boy to dangerous cities

Nothing on this raging mother took pity
She wails for justice night & day
then conjures up a wrathful lady beast
who has a rooster in her heart
The stick! The stick! Is it
the prick or spine or scourge of
mother's love?

## Colors

*for M.H.*

"*I sing of times trans-shifting, and I write
How roses first came red and lilies white.*"
— ROBERT HERRICK

Colors are more complicated than a state
        of concentration & rest, or state of
expansion & speed. Take your pick.
        Ask one whose equilibrium is broken yet
her colors surround you: optimum blue,
        heart's blood, green in every nerve.
You rush to the window — what goes on
        out there? Yellow sits you down on
time & listens, while white is saved
        for later. We blur, not restraining
ourselves, & disappear: white onto white.
        Alfred "Ubu Roi" Jarry was said to drink
red ink with his dinner to startle his
        companions. They clutched their abdomens
in dismay. I whited out your name from
        the text when So & So entered the room.
Her hands yellowed with age & the bleating
        habit of opium. Green with obduracy,
love turns to hate & withers. But
        I save blue to wrap you in, dear reader,
blue as yesterday's ether. Compose
        your world. A mind jumps into successive
states that become inseparable companions
        which blend or curdle as wind churns
the bowl. Add this, erase that. He has a
        lot of grey on tonight. I wear black
to celebrate the death of color. She is
        my aqua-nemesis. You mix & paint from
your own palette, see natural harmonies
        & witness night to dawn shift in the
self-existing chromo-kingdom. Do you
        remember? You & I were small in the
color hierarchy with our restless bodies
        our red desire, green aspiration.

## Out There

You say
This is all
there is
I say
nothing much
to help
Say this
Say what?
It is
what you say
it is
And it is
everything
You teach me
this is
all there is
And this is
all there is
is everything
A night back
there where
a head
is turning
to kiss air
is all there is
is everything
Out there
stars are dark
The motel is quiet
Bob
One of the colors
is missing
from our world

## Lindsay Speaks

I like it when it's spring
When the trees grow & when flowers grow
I like it because then fences are things you can climb on
You can climb them it's not so snowy
You can play outside more
Clouds are white, the sky is blue
& spring is pretty you can play outside more
I like tulips growing because I like the smell of flowers
You can play on trees, climb on them
maybe if you have strong enough shoes
I've got tennis shoes, leather shoes & jelly shoes
I like jellies because you can see my pretty toenails
Bees suck the air out of tulips
But they don't live in them
Nothing lives in tulips but water
The sun goes behind the clouds to the other part of the earth
I would say sky is "up there"
and moon is white up there.

# Romance

SHE
Born & lost in a throw of time
I'm always thinking of shunning time
because I change my mind or dress so often
Cerulean: for your eyes
Amber beads at dawn, a lilting surface
whose light makes eyes fiery as if silenced
ideas would suddenly be released out of head
Color would jump at an offer, wouldn't you?
Disjointed dreams owned by a Capitalist:
my glistening black shoulders entering armchairs
A petrified thought so I'll stop talking
and you speak

LOVER
Your yokel ambition to be many of face
& all seduction will halt my laziness
If wanton eyes change, please look this way
Come 'round the bend and any woman
you'd care to be is fine with me,
we're unfeasible in a crowd, however
and as dusk approaches let's zigzag outta here
Compensations exist in the landscape
and shouldn't be exploited a great deal
like patches of snow don't really
sabotage romance, do they? Who are you?
Can you breathe, attired flamboyantly?

SHE
Ideals are noble but you are
dressed to give a more modern touch
to the room, although you rankle me
the way you are young & require purification
You sound me out because afternoon
gives me desire. I could be somber
if a light rain would fall, I could be
utilized if you'll mountain climb
anywhere in this Capitalist joint

& forgive the scheme of asking dumb questions
I'm not so deficient. Kiss me

LOVER
Protein? Vengeance? Jealousy?
We ought to get out together more often
It's hard to explain how austerity
gets in your bones. I am the child of
one of you & it's easy to be taken in:
Into all probability, into the years on end,
into a liberation struggle, into a persistent
pattern and my heart (which should be studying)
breaks for you, for love of you
In this way you are making me love
a sumptuous ill-afforded item,
or lead me through premature twilight

SHE
In this way I'll be appealing:
Form is joy! In this way, all of me
will enter the lounge as if no one ever
starved or suffered, as if no one reads anymore
as if that in itself could scare me, as
if we are all economic exploiters coated in oil
As if I could enter one room for the rest of life,
aloof, tight-lipped I can hardly breathe
being more abandoned than usual,
more than what you say, more than what
you ever say, it's automatic

WIND IN FOOTHILLS
Automatically dramatic, dominating
and side by side with lavish texture & style
You could always do this & are liberated —
No going back! The wind says: You
are amusing & therefore the wind moves for you,
spins for you and won't settle easily tonight
Wind can be rueful too, and stubborn
not behaving like any government.

## The Cure

Who I was & what I wanted & what I did & what happened
  & whose every air was you could say something
    like corruption, something like a willful collaboration:
    a full cup. Something was a wilderness with us
      It kept us in feeling & was a wit in a dungeon
        & I was a mass of hair & nails for you, foolhardy as
          our passion was inconvenient all the time, so much swept
            aside to please you who are wanting more, no one is satisfied

And under this cloud of evil, what talks? What moves to
  make me obtain advice? What course to follow?
    Another fair incognita throws herself at your feet & you
      must answer without delay, not a patronage to turn a back
        for this is not to blame either. Should I dress myself as a page
        and follow secretly like the heroine of Lara?
          No these are not those times, no these are not those times
            The words are reflected as by a mirror back to you

Behavior is only hinted at by the student of the human mind
  who says this and wants to separate us from the hypnotic power
    of your eyes. You the romantic who stalks the school
      with a pseudonym of the cavalier, and is not a shock to
        one so ridden with energy she likes to stomp and shout
          But when she gives it all, does she give at all? The
          heart's at low ebb & love is against the will of one
            who was the quaint name for a tendency, not a human being

For we are playthings of the stars who mock us or rather
  they care not, being models of patience themselves
    How to speak of them? Of it? Of our assignation? How to
      be a rash innocent all over again, not a young thing
        but marching on in time, Napoleon into Russia: a disaster?
          What a shrinking situation in the next act, what a glow
            to put on, the rolling of the industrial Star Wars snowball
              which waltzes us along with it, clearing the roots of fate

But what is the price, dashing off a few new verses?
  What ink gets diluted in space, what scathing coruscations
    of new particular midage genius. The star ascends
      & others are welcome too to make sense of these theses
        that the world doesn't belong to anyone per se
          My thinking is like a ship freighted with long travel
            & duties to pay and be done. Not affording to mince words
              yet make merry with them & can't escape with me as hussy

Not to lose all enthusiasm for matrimony but rather a contrary
  arrangement, the poem can be tender enough O here is a child
    in the poem too! O here is my inflated heart, O my first
      sight of you, a family man, and everywhere to answer these critics
        with the caprice of a literate, & some seasoned fuel to plead
          this case & amplify the working title which is not
            a pulsing retreat sort of one but the name of an element
              that resonates with plutonium & grabs the air & throat of you

& who you are & what you wanted & what you did & learn a lesson
  about pre-existence, a huckster calling too loudly for anyone's ears a
    tribunal in the family business, a hopeful idealist, a way
      to not sever all ties all raging so that one is not an
        endangered species in this relationship. It's cloudy out here
          the trees are barely visible, my conscience walks the heath,
            I have not healed, I'll shelter the miscreant & wade through
              any bog. What century is it? Did we progress at all? What's

in it for the future bunglers? They are trying out a new set of keys
  tonight & struggling long after dawn. It is a small mountain
    town that beckons you because in it you gave birth to a prince
      of hope & beauty. He was engaged to remind you that this other
        love wills itself along and the species is tenacious so
          do not widen the chasm between us. Can a mother speak so
            directly? Will the boy never be quiet? And share this
              news with actual experience. Elections arise & sticks of names

flower on everyone's lawn. A man whose worth is not in question
who seems opportunistic to some as he appears on television thrives &
might do anything to get elected: why? Will do anything, why?
A distant connection to be self-appointed and an epistle of
moderation which reeks of power rather than the perfectibility
of man which could be spoken of in more dulcet tones & opinions
like a rose shedding its luster goes on & on. In a belief
system still sweet kisses are there, rapture is there

& do not spare me any confrontation sexual or otherwise for
I love to unbar my body & my heart, not a painted angel,
not hiding behind this old machine whose elements suffer
around punctuation, and huffs along like my train of thinking
saying Do not resort to violence, do not resort to dwelling in
the pain of this face & heart, and celebrate those days
you walked like any other, and rode in a car like a novice,
it was the turn in your life to do this. It was the cure.

## Ballade:

*"Par amour n'aim, ne amer ne voudroie"*

after CHRISTINE DE PISAN

My heart's felt no wounds big or small
from Cupid's darts, which they say
make war on many
I've not—Thank God!—been caught
in the booby trap of prison
of the God of Love
I make him no pleas but live alone in delight
I have no lover I don't want one

& I'm not afraid of being caught
by smouldering looks fancy gifts or hot chase
or trapped by wheedling words
There's no man can match my heart
Let none come after me for help
I'll turn him off saying
Nay, I have no lover & I don't want one

& I'll laugh at any woman
caught in such stupid peril
She should have killed herself long ago
She's lost all honor in the world
I intend to live my whole life
in this state & say to all who entreat me
I have no lover I don't want one

Prince of Love, what on earth
should I do at your court?
Nay, I have no lover I don't want one!

## Sonnet: O Husband!

O Husband! this word of care born &
possible serenity, of kingship, of
intimations of property. You husband me,
do I wife you? Is this a marriage of
roles & names? If husband, you I should
honor & obey & if I don't, what recourse —
to break asunder? Let it be marriage of
bottom natures — between two stable points —
the heaven of you, the earth of me
Or is it insult to stretch the boundary?
Don't rage or jealous be when I enjoin
to you the true most stretched heart of me
"me" who is less solid being than
ever wont to be, but that's the truth
as through meditation & poetry we see & as
I'm a woman, am empty, yet full of light for thee.

## 3 Epiphanies

What ever happened to
Hermie Giuffre?
We took our clothes off
on the upper screened porch
of the green house grandfather
built before the War
It was raining
My small brother hid
behind a rocking chair
I guess what I was thinking
was how different I am
from that boy, and
What's wrong with that?
The word "naked," the word "penis"

*

The storm rocked us
My companion went crazy
thinking he was Lord Randall
crawling with eels,
poisoned by his mother
He held me down, first time,
talked smoothly about sex
His hair & skin were luminous
I thought of him as "saint,"
"victim," "mad"
He was like a twin brother
all golden    I saw myself
as Medieval sun-girl
He taught me pleasure,
the meaning of "heart's sorrow"

*

In the Winter dream
I had a son named A-Man,
who could speak in tongues
When the nurse, in life, said
"It's a girl," I knew she was wrong
He cut me like a man.

## Philosophia Perennis

I turned: quivering yellow stars in blackness
I wept: how speech may save a woman
The picture changes & promises the heroine
That nighttime & meditation are a mirage

To discuss pro & contra here is mute
Do I not love you, day?
A pure output of teleological intentions
& she babbles, developing a picture-theory of language

Do I not play the delicate game of language?
yes, & it is antecedent to the affairs of the world:
The dish, the mop, the stove, the bed, the marriage
& surges forth the world in which I love

I and I and I and I and I and I, infinitely reversible
Yet never secure in the long morning texture
A poor existing woman-being, accept her broken heart
& yet the earth is divinity, the sky is divinity
The nomads walk & walk.

## Face the Orient

MORTAL EYES
I need to be dancing over the birth
of children, something with a crocodile
head, hippo body, lion's feet, and then
there's the dwarf with luxuriant beard,
leopard's tail & crooked legs, presiding
over attire.

OTHER CULTURE
Dress me up too! I'd swallow the key
forever if I could. I'd be a self-
concluding thing, a stream-flow.
Penetrate me if you can.

MORTAL  EYES
You sound the jealous god! Metals
shimmer. Colors glow. Tones sing.
& now I'm speaking in a word, to
name you & make you bloom. You have
your sweetness I beg & I'll wager my
posture on it. I stand up so as to
see better; maybe I'm just pretending
to think.

OTHER CULTURE
Thinking gives you solipsistic ideas, ask
me. And drown into another system. Keep
your deities & jars and honeycomb. Keep
your spools & wheelings & calendars. I've got
my own.

MORTAL EYES
I'm brought up to use these words, utter
sound, think your thoughts, all the while
looking up as if something's up there.
Is there? Time is a spiral & dreams me
up. Is there? Is there?

OTHER CULTURE
I try to use the dream too

MORTAL EYES
Is there & does it love? And crawl? Does
it crawl first? Is it born?

OTHER CULTURE
Like the warpath, like the giant, like
the mirror, like the tomb, like the book
in my thinking. Look in here and read.
Look here. The horizon is the book.

c

## Poeme en Forme de la Bouche

Night first settles in the     corners of your mouth
Mouth quotes philosophers quid pro quo, pronounces vocables
upon the hour & represents a state of kissing pilgrims call a
a parts-of-the-body-whirr speech. Moth travels, mouth never bypasses
cities. Mouth is awake.         Vatic  silence from
Biloxi to Aberdeen to         Winnipeg to bedsitting
rooms. Mouth opens        the  day,  gulps  the
scheme, is built        into  receiving line
of  machines,        bytes,  infinitesimal
allowances,        still    talking,
talking. Misunderstood as nourishment, disturbs the house, conflicts
with voters, is not to be believed, swells the duets, oracles are
vast rambling speeches. O MOUTH: Swallow the night!

214

## from *Iovis Omnia Plena*

> He catches my eye, my fancy
> October
> I ride an orange car
> The radio is sad & hopeful
> "Don't Turn Your Back on Love"
> Clouds lift higher
> & clutter the mountain
> It's in the weather everywhere
> I am helpless
> Ex Stasis
> I'm Gaia
> Father Sky look down on me
> Stars are his eyes
> He enters me
> All is full of him

What's true by excluding nothing (I can't really do this): the birth-place, the rain (40 days & 40 nights) observed from a screen porch. Cradle me in memory and make me a goddess-fearing Titan. I didn't resist & pulled my weight, a firecracker to be born in this world. And swept in the tide of this post-war boom, the child of such & such a divine mother and a father, the soul of gentleness. A plain kind of basics weep now to think of modesty in financial matters & hard facts of life, the fanatical enemy war that made sense, the war that hoped to be brought into a safer place, the letters and photographs, you can imagine, & description of dead soldier limbs lifted out of rubble (he saw this, they saw this, they all saw this) the unmitigated trouble of it, and it a mighty cause, and the children everywhere of it now, in my life, of survivors, prisoners, dead ones, tortured or heroic, what could come after this in the nuclear sense? Yet how it "ended," what is the payoff, the result of any way you look at it, those survivors too, the Japanese, and now we live in the combined kar-ma, if I might use that word, dear sister dear Yoshiko, dear reader dear student, in the sense of what continues, a thread of energy perhaps is all. Which is why now I can say the poet must be a warrior of the battlefield of Mars, o give me a break, thank you very much.

No one will sign on this dotted sky line. But what is perceived is the vast body, the sky itself, coupled with earth and someone (Virgil) said: IOVIS OMNIA PLENA. All is full of Jove (his sperm presumably to people Chaos).

> Whole the moon, whole the year
>   tuliz  U  tuliz  hab
> whole the day, whole the night,
>   tuliz  kin  tuliz  akab
> whole the breath when it moved too, whole the blood too
>   tuliz ik cu ximbal xan   tuliz kik xan
> when they came to their beds     their mats, their thrones;
>   tu kuchul tu uayob tu poopoob tu dzamob
> rhythm in their reading of the good hours,
>   ppiz u caxanticob yutzil kin
> as they observed the good stars enter their reign,
>   la tu ppiz yilcob yocolob yahaulil utzul ekob tu yahaulil
> Everything was good
>   Utz tun tulacal

But this is way after the feminine principle is making her mark on universal time equals space. I don't know anything, I know it all. The war is full of war and Levite laws, not tamed by laws of mercy, and Astoreth goes underground, as women are dragged into caves. And later a cruel Gentile world. Research: intercourse with mothers & daughters (as beasts do) a dream:

This was after the fall of the mother earth & giants
I said this already about sweetness
I said My Father, like a small lake
"Creators" as in Greek for poets, yet nothing is created from limitless mind
but
but this

> The famous artist takes me to a hotel in a city like Portland. I'm a real redhead now, but am concerned about the Dharma test I had to take earlier & I have the distinct feeling they'll say I was

216

being too literal when I wrote the phrase "Things as they are." I was thinking, then, on the phrase, how I wouldn't have a daughter now that I had all these "I"s. Two boy children, where did the second come from? Red is now pulling the black slip strap down. I am excited but worried about his exotic girlfriend who is brewing Vietnamese coffee in the next room. "Wait don't move!" He says as we're about to kiss. "Hold that stance!" He pours a bag of cement in the robin's-egg blue porcelain sink, mixing it with hot water the way you do henna. Then he picks up a little shovel in front of the fireplace and proceeds to dump the mixture over my head. It feels good and quells desire.

but this desire

is a weekend

a mere idea

I think "50 labels self-sticking"

I think how life is compounded by paper

I think how sleep tonight tomorrow you suffer

I think I'll fall in love with him all over again

Me a Woodswoman from the City of the Mill

Grandfather John a glassblower, sedate in the wind,

spectacled, pale, works hard in the Protestant ethic


Millville, New Jersey, which was the epitome of a place small

& human and at the lake the motorboat coming in at dusk.

There was a swing piano style (my father's)

& the chimney he (a father) built on the house never to

be owned ours

Millville, Feb 4, 1902

My Darling,

Yours at hand — and I would certainly have been disappointed if I had not received it. I have been resting a little since supper — as I am real tired tonight it is now nearly seven o'clock and we go to German lessons at eight. I hope you have spent two real nice pleasant days and hope the remainder of the week is or will be just the same and also that you derive lots of good from them. Now my first two days have not been so pleasant I have had some real trials nothing has went well and I feel real out of sorts tonight. I hardly know what I would have done had I not received a letter from someone very precious to me. Well our orders have been running very bad lately. I think things will come better hereafter I hope so anyway. Well this is too much grumbling for you I won't complain any more.

I went out to Church last night. James wanted me to help him sing Well they had a very good meeting. I think there were two conversions. The young man who they tried to get Sunday night his brother was converted, he was there but would not go but they think he will tonight. May McLaughlin's father was up last night. Mr. Hunter asked that the men invite all of the men in the factory tonight and I think there will be a big time there. Mrs. Hunter is going to sing Memories tonight.

Well I am going to finish up on scolding. Now who said it would do good to be apart awhile I would like to know did I ever say that and mean it? Oh yes! You ought to see my mustache it's a beauty. Well darling feed up well and when you come home Sallie will soon kill the fatted calf. Don't worry about me going skating. No more for me. Remember me to all I will close and go learn a little dutch

Yours only and truly

John W. Waldman

Admonishing students to avoid writing the grandmother
in the attic, for example, or mother too, think of Creeley &
that respect & ease
To ease the distant dead one
But the mother was hard on the father, dominating 47 MacDougal
Street you must say "below Houston"


A: So talk a little bit about your neighborhood.

R: We're passing the new Golden Pacific National Bank which
is kind of a outstanding piece of Chinese architecture, very
brand-new. And it's already beginning to flake off on the red
columns. And they've got outside marble Chinese dragons and
we're heading now past the old Centre Street main police station
which has been abandoned for ten years, but is about to be
opened up as a condominium. And I think it'll be quite a land-
mark. Now we're, as we get to the corner of Broome and Centre
Street, we're looking across to what I believe to be a German-
sponsored project which seems also to be some sort of condo-
minium, I...

A: ...are wacky...this green...

R: Yeah, well that's the old stuff. The building itself has some
kind of, it's kind of nice, it looks like ... I don't know what it looks
like, but...

A: Yeah, but the windows could be a little?

R: Yeah, but the new design is, for some reason, somebody
chose this kind of aluminum siding ...

A: Look at that chandelier, I mean, it's so odd...

R: Right. And they didn't put anything over their awning there.

A: Germans you said?

R: For some reason, I don't know why, I heard that Germans had
taken over the place. Now we're getting up to Cleveland Place
and we're passing Eileen's Cheesecake which is a very distin-
guished product, I certainly sponsor it.

A: Where? Not this.

R: No. We just passed Eileen's. Now we're getting up past the old methadone center, which is now moved up here, which was kind of an outrage in the neighborhood. We're passing Jennifer Bartlett's loft. She was very much against the methadone clinic. Now we're getting even to the fire station and past PIM magazine, a very cute little miniature gallery, which is also the publisher of probably the smallest publication in New York. And we're heading now past the illustriously renovated Puck Building.

A: And what's the story on the Puck Building?

R: Well, the Puck Building was for years and years like a printed ink building. They manufactured printing ink. And it always smelled very nicely. But since some big entrepreneur has taken it over and done a nice job, it looks pretty glamorous. They've got green trees out here, anti-bum fences and I think they rent out the ground floor to benefits, big dos, you know. I think Williwear had a do there or something. I don't know who else, but lots of things and probably there's some terrific spaces there. Now right here we're on the corner of Houston and Centre Street or Lafayette Street as it turns, it turns into Lafayette and then turns into Park Avenue, and we're in what I think is filling-station land, where all the cabbies gas up at the gaseteria here, it's an Amoco station on my left. And across the street is the fast parking, gas-and-wash emporium, which is probably the best place to get your car washed around here. And then there's the attractive Lafayette Tire and Auto Safety Center, sporting a Michelin tire sign and looking pretty jazzy. And there you see the remains of an old City Walls mural. It looks kinda like from Byzantine days. And now we're just passing Houston Street and there's many — Houston Street still is holding about the same pattern with some slight gentrification to the west here, with some new stores on the SoHo side. And now we're heading down, we're heading west on Houston Street, just passing the car wash place. Not much to say about that I haven't already said. Across the street you see the billboard for the Semaphore Gallery which I think is quite interesting, they are changing it every month and doing a nice presentation with a new billboard by the artist they're showing at that, concurrently. That's pretty interesting.

A: That's one of a kind, isn't it?

R: Yeah, I don't know any other gallery that does that. I mean, they, and they only do it at one billboard. And I saw an artist there for the first time that I liked a lot, and then I went to see the show, so it worked on me. Now we're, we just, we're just almost in the heart of SoHo, we're just about to pass, we're passing these new stores. The first of them seems to be called Fuel Injection, which I think is a Japanese, sort of fast-food clothing boutique. And, what's happening, this is the old Lilien Hardware and Supply Co. on the northwest corner. That's been there forever.

Cabbie: Forget about that fifty cents, I hit that by mistake.

R: Right. Thank you. Now, this part of Houston, oh this is a very interesting natural park by I think the artist's name is Sonfist, What's his name, Alan?

A: That sounds right, now you've confused me.

R: Something like that. But it's a very nice experiment to get the landscape exactly back to its natural state. Letting, even letting the weedlike structures come in to play. Now we're passing the Italian, which one is this called?

A: St. Anthony's.

R: Yeah. St. Anthony's. So, I mean, food festival.

A: It's where I grew up. Right here.

R: Thompson Street?

A: Two houses down. The grey house, the red one. I grew up on the top floor.

R: Wow. Doesn't look like it changed much. Are you Italian?

A: No. I wish. No, I'm a Protestant, a Huguenot.

R: And you grew up there?

A: Yeah. I grew up there. My father still lives there.

R: Wow. I didn't know that.

A: My brother's living there now. Forty-seven MacDougal. The St. Anthony's parochial school is across the street, I grew up in the festa and I went to school right on King Street.

R: . . . Canal Street, it's like a forty-dollar number or something.

221

A: Really. I'll go get one. I have about three at once. They're broken down.

R: Yeah. Go to Canal Street.

A: Which place?

R: It was near, well, they got so many of them. This place happened to be near Centre Street on the north side, very near the corner. On the street, like out at, you know, on a table outside. Now we're into what is really kind of a backwash. I mean, we're near a Martin's bar and I think almost all—

A: (can't hear)  bar.

R: Oh, yeah, the sob. Actually, I've never been in there, have you?

A:  No.

R: Is that like a club, nightclub? Music loft?

A: Yeah. Music loft.

R: But I know this Martin's bar across the way, which is at Varick, and is this Houston?

A:  Yeah.

R: Has been there from year one. And I think almost all Martin's bars were, used to like, be all over the City, or have been torn down or changed.

A: There's a loft for rent.

R: That loft, that loft has been for rent for twenty-five years. I have for years, I have speculated living there for years. Because it's always for rent.

Cabbie:  (can't hear)

A: What's that?

Cabbie:  They open after-hours places in these lofts now.

A: Open air . . .

R: They're after-hours clubs.

A: Oh, after-hours clubs.


The cabbie hinted no subject matter but the experience of that father going to school on the G.I. Bill, studying that beautiful language of literature, & that was that & could attain right

222

livelihood in such a manner of speaking, and nailed on the oilcloth to the black table my mother's first husband built with half-Grecian hand upon which we had countless meals and struggles. And Glaukos surfaced once to defend a poor Mexican, be beaten up alive still, hospitalized, too gentle in this New York world.

Welcome in this world, Met Opera broadcasts and hiding places behind awkward chairs and fear of oranges from the little brother who came into this world to make me jealous & wiser. My father on the post-war dream, recovering, come on get with it, not a Catholic in me, although we are surrounded and informed and made alive by these visions and rituals & food. I did *too* see the Devil with the rest of them in the girls' room at P.S. 8! I swear, Mrs. Mulherne! He was red with horns & a tail & a sneer & he smelled like the devil too, all spermy & peppery. You could say he was a sex symbol, a voyeur (we were so little, prepubescent in the long lunchroom hour). The older half-Greek half-brother confused me with his little black box, Pandora's he called it, a box of woes, the accoutrement of the diabetic. How many relationships to break a heart? This is for fathers & brothers. A younger golden boy who usurped the breast, the remote father, tamed by war, the mysterious half-Greek, a dark musician. I honor & obey these first men in my life who were to repeat in a swirl of patterns & combinations of other men so dear to me. Should I go on?


President Ronald Reagan
The White House
1600 Pennsylvania Avenue, N.W.
Washington, D.C. 20500

Dear Mr. President:

On November 19 and 20, when you meet with General Secretary Gorbachev in Geneva, the hopes of not just all Americans, but of the entire world, will be with you.

Mr. President, I believe that we must take steps to limit the nuclear arms race.

I recognize that the Soviets are our principal adversaries in the world. They are tough, determined negotiators. Nevertheless, each of your last five predecessors—Presidents Kennedy, Johnson, Nixon, Ford, and Carter—has been able to work out important nuclear arms control treaties with them—treaties which have helped reduce the threat of nuclear war.

The Geneva summit provides you with a real chance to break the current negotiating impasse—to reach the kind of agreement between leaders which is needed to obtain significant arms control.

As you yourself have said, "A nuclear war cannot be won and must never be fought."

Mr. President, now is the time to put the power of your high office behind those important and telling words. Now is the time to take positive steps to limit the nuclear arms race.

The Geneva summit represents an opportunity to break the arms control stalemate of the last five years and to enact new arms control limits which will *strengthen*—not weaken—our national security.

I encourage you to seize the opportunity the Geneva summit offers.

Sincerely,

Anne-Who-Grasps-The-Broom-Tightly

June 1, 1904

My Dear

I just finished reading your letter and I will say you are rather late in the day to have a bouquet holder made by Saturday. Why tomorrow is Thursday and it would be Sat. before it would come out of the oven. You should have thought of this sooner. You can get one later if you wish. I am very sorry I did not send you the measure for those windows right. But I will get them for you tonight and will mail this letter when I return home. The number on the house is 419. I am very sorry you are having such bad weather but I think it will be clear tomorrow. I understand Mr. Ware to say you told him about the carpet. I will give Mr. Sithers your note tomorrow. Will finish this when I return home tonight.

Well it is now nine o'clock I have been uptown I went out to the house The measure of the windows from centre to bottom of casing is 39 inches. I hardly think the number I told you above is correct It is 417 but I will explain. The double house next to it on the west side is 411 & 413 so I think ours should be 417 but the single house on the east side is 423 There is no number on the house as yet. You have them printed 417. They have 2 rooms papered downstairs — they look real nice Well I will close now hoping that I have everything alright

Ever your John

November 21, '85

Dear Anne,

You tell all and remain mysterious. You've got love to burn. The poem floors me, the words cut me up. Ardent and mute, yes, I am. The dancing does it, but I can't tell, can't speak; I worry, a conscience violated? Afraid of loss, so always losing. Patterns emerge: the legs, a certain shape, the butt, breast, firm, proportion, most important, but aura, it's everything, inseparable. The temptation of one who wants more attack.

In La Jolla, the Pacific is Mediterranean blue. The museum's windows look out on it, and the art isn't as good. George Trakas, know him? he's renovating a hill there. We dance in the theatre. We flew over you, both ways, and I wanted to stop and ask you how to make life-enhancing love out of this passion-pain.

Your son's becoming a demon perhaps? I and my son, possessed by demons, must become them.

Thanks for the passionate communication. I love you.

> Son: We are lovers & Daddy is a wolf
> How old are you Mommy? 44? 29?
> Mommy you are always 21. Come
> down to 21 Mommy. Stay 21 forever
> & I'll grow up to 21. You are
> not as loud as Dad. You have no
> scratchy face. You are my most
> beautiful Mommy.

I get out & am not a sneaking Madam
Not a silhouette
Not a dreamy housekeeper
Not writing the modern Arcadia
Tangibly not at home
The copy on this page, on my shelves, in my heart
    in my room is not a lie
Not mere loneliness, not slipshod
Not metrical, but operating
as pioneer, as trust, as Woman
as Passion, as Champion of Details


My older brother's wife rips up the photograph of his earlier daughter. I struggle in heart with the little godchild my lover commands with him into my world. The male makes us suffer for his heart of hearts. I sleep with my older brother's brother not my blood but who yet resembles him, after sitting on my brother's lap in what seems like a long taxi ride (it was raining) home. My mother is trying to keep us apart. We go to Hotel Earle with old man lobby, whore at the door and make illicit love something like incest, unskilled in a burning urge to forge a link. The beautiful god is in town a few days, heading out west. Can I really make love to this yet again another Greek? Too cerebral, unsatisfied. It's the dark connection in this one. I always wore a black turtleneck then. I speak confidently.

The blond on the telephone is a long story, like my younger another brother who confesses desire for drugs & men. He takes my virginity as we used to say and we are cheerful in a sullied bed. Because my mother died I can speak these things I state again this is for fathers, brothers, lovers, husbands, son for that is next of kin alive & changing in a fluid world. It is a palpable motion towards them from one who slumbered many years in the body of a man and in herself a turf of woman becoming Amazonian in proportions (I grow larger even as I write this) as she spans a continent takes on the wise mother as she dies. I gave birth to a son to better understand the men whose messages pour out of me.

Dear Iovis:

Thinking about you: others in you & the way
You are the sprawling male world today
You are also the crisp light in another day
You are the plan which will become clearer with a
     strong border as you are the guest, the student
You are the target
You are the border you are sometimes the map
You are in a car of love
You are never the enemy, dull & flat, dissolving in the sea
Illusion lays its snare, you resort to bait, to tackle me
Our day is gone
To name a place steeped in legend is tempting
To name now and then Nambikwari, Arawak, Poona, makes
     them appear
We go as far as possible, any old town disappears
We look at the globe from vantage point of sun
The clouds under us are rich with
For manners for trouble for passion we do this to each other
     & forces us back into not-so-terrible childhood
     & forward to old age sickness death you know it
The lines translate to Sanskrit as I say this to you
Exhaustion with phenomena at last
As I say this to you the furniture is rearranged in a sacred text
The room is now long, the room is tall, the room is male
It is a cathedral after you have named them all for me
Or Theodora, a lusty woman
It is All Hallows' Eve & many dead lovers walk tonight
The wind goes through us, we aren't so solid
All you could hold onto I'm knocking out of you
The wind did this when I wasn't looking to me too
Your conscious eyes compel us together
A game of guesses
What is in the gentleman's mind?
Something in you reminds me of a magnate, a planet, a small prayer
A little girl is trapped inside trying to get out of you
I make a new plan every day to ride your mind
Drugs are inconvenient & stand outside the room
In the other room, the "she" carries it off, waving goodbye
The great thing is to love something

the land, the sea, the sweep of a hand, the way something boils
Man is the arm gesture of the woman or something like that says T.
The battle with the "Ugly Spirit" is not to be discounted says D.
A. needed a woman and caressed a tree
B. knows maximum intensity is best in this life
A world of heredity quiet in R.'s syllables
A woman's mockery is strong & hearty
She's fond of knowledge learn something about her
The large heart scans the future
Vague unrest I tell you so
You contradict your many selves
Your mind spills out, the page holds on
"You make a man of me" sings radio, gruffly

All is full of Jove, he fucks everything
It is the rough way to prove it
The male gods descend & steal power
How does it happen
How does it happen Blanche Fleur & Heart Sorrow?

Here's how:

I lie back & take him in. He wounds me after a fashion. A new sensation of art & stimulus, for I watch them both & participate after a fashion until they are spent & the man is melted in arms, and no longer to do battle on this bed stage. The bed is the book is the bed is the book where sheets record every muscle tear sweat ooze of life & groan. It is the playground of the senses for this artist as sweet rehearsal for the nonexistent pages that will honor this rumbling & panic and lostness. I want to say to dear male lovers living & dead not anger made this but with due respect in spite of the crimes of which your sex is prone. I honor the member who is a potential wand of miracles, who dances for his supper, who is the jester & fool and sometimes the saint of life. But she, me, who takes it, who responds clasping with cunt teeth, the receiver, the mountain, whatever it could be called, the emptying, the joining of this most radiant sphere where the chakras glow under the sheets or else they are fucking in water, she is witness in this brave act. It feels like the great sperm whale entered me.

II.

Mature love you say but my wounds come out through inner temple

which are participants containing a statue of . . . female personnel,

not subject matter, a tableau of outerspace, concubines?

where we had countless meals and struggles with any father.

What is the mature and conditioned space O Jove?


Dear Anne,

Please advise how I may develop a scintillating poetic presence,
Last time I read most dozed off. I dislike Virgil. Result of having to
construe 40 lines a day at Choate — those endless similes

> As when at dawn the ducks
> from out the marsh
> Curdling their pintails in
> the early starch
> etc etc etc

Sorry, that's clammy armpit . . .

Very best to all,

JL


Never liked Jove either. Wd prefer to be inhabited
by Αφρωδιτη or some nifty Olympian girl.

It is a play or way to amuse the girl or is it? A way to talking
is another to journey to never abuse but wounds are fake and
are the scourge of me and they are real scourge of me. Where
to leave off talk of all these brothers and leave it here.
Dear  Man-Who-Rends-My-Table-And-My-Hearth: SCRAM!

Dear  Man-Who-Rends-My-Table-And-My-Hearth:  SCRAM!
I am a ruined table because
I met a maiden good
I walked into an explicit house
and was a trait of forefathers
They could arrest me in my cunning
But they are not the boss of me
They are not the actor in
a new phase of history: horse & chariot
They are not a grimace in this old gal's boot
We are like one city and another
And another comes along soon
the shape of Neptune's face
or Saigon, a sight for the broken
heart of anything
It is the ancient place of Ur
It is your own place won in fair fight
giving the lie to property tax
and the language of my people
O Male Civilizations!
I am not a party to my gold
but relate what has gone past
once the sufferings are over
Are they ever? I doubt it
But they are done to a crisp
and die in cold light
I am a regular next winter
I am a vestal in my propensity for service
I stretch my neck with music
but I doubt the way The Prophet
goes about bringing them to the Mount
Not doubt but a kind of wonder
It is a fiery night
and proud Maisie stalks the wood
She is the maiden of me
She is the good of me
I am a timetable for anything wet,
for anything with star and waxing moon
I am the dream of me, mere
illusory scales & fins, webbed toes
I grow into the scout of me

230

the densest one who reports back
to the head of me and sprouts
the garden you put your mind to
one sunny day
It glows like a pregnant thing
and grows the seed of any Art
It is alive nor is
the heart of me dead
I go so that a windless bower be built
So that I go quietly, I go alone
I am alone and delight in how speech
may save a woman
How speech is spark of intrusion


LETTER TO MISS IDONA HAND

Washington July 15, 1903

My Dear

I suppose you rec'd a postal from me by Tuesday noon—I
thought you would be anxious to know weather we arrived safely
or not. We have had a splendid time. I cannot describe the beauti-
ful sights we have seen it is something wonderful. I and the boys
are sitting in the Pennsylvania depot. They are waiting while I
write this small message. We just saw the house where Garfield
was shot. We have covered a good bit of ground since arriving but
we have several places yet to visit. I am trying to make a note of
everything so I can explain it to you. But next summer you must
see things for yourself. This is the most beautiful place I ever saw.
Everybody is feeling well we have a few jokes on one another.
When we first arrived we walked down Sixth Street and we want-
ed 452. Charlie looked and saw the number 859 and called it out.
It was a sign saying established 1859. You want to ask him if he
stopped on Establishment Street. This morning I awoke about 6
o'clock their was a bell ringing it rang twice and then commenced
ringing harder. I said Boys their is a fire. I lit out of bed in a hurry.
They are having fun about that. Well Dear I must close now hop-

ing this will do you some little good. I will be home about Saturday and tell you all about it.

yours

John


What are you you are what are you are you what seems lady?
Idona's seamed stockings in the attic, John a Protestant
never protesting on the porch, a gentle man outside any
war, born in the gap between worlds in collision.
All the lovers getting out of the army for one sane reason
or another, generation skipped. The grandfather in white,
father in khaki I won't skip over them to what you are
You're a pistol eye a mistletoe a missile man a Marxist
You're a sword eye a job queen a devil-may-care
You're a conch a knob you guys are slobs
We're playing ticktacktoe you're a sticky glue-stick
but a stick-in-the-mud too are you
You're spaghetti-hair Dad, you crazy old man
You woman Daddy you *New York Times* reader
You *New York Times* reporter
You're a suitcase  What? What are you?
You're east of the sun & west of the moon
Are you are you are you are you   What? What are you?
You slob you rubber band nose
You're a bully and a mean-shoot a paper clip a peppercorn
You've stuck in my teeth
You're a European walrus
You're a blue muscle you're a red tomato
You crossbow you arrowhead you man-of-me
You're a bellow of church
You're a bump thump bump dummy
You're a broken-down hospital

you're a cracked people
You're craggy rock cliff
You're Michael Jackson you're Jacky Frosty
You cup nothing
You're a hundred thousand bristle blocks
you're a peony—means you're a broken-down housebell
You are my wife Mommy you are the dream of me


        The keep & key of an unruly person
        absorbed everyone & you realize he's
        only wild since noon

You're just out there looking at the moon

        So great my love on my male partners
        I have to leave town

(When you look into it on any person's desk
the town appears small)

        so now

I RISE BEFORE ISHTAR IN THE EAST
I RISE BEFORE ISHTAR IN THE EAST

Moon  disappearing
all's sluggish, dull
What's the color
Pronounce it windless
A shroud song is sad
sword cuts  who?
Some wicker man staggers
Listen to the peregrine fall
I try, towered upon a short stretch
Seeing Mother meshed with herself
O dire is her Mother need
She's shortened loose
She's in the fittings

Windows iced into dark holes
are quiet
but I think of a dream
in green jasper
It goes like this:
something shattered in chips
sailing down      (was it?)
long canals
cut channels
Something like Hawaii
for the craft
Need sharp eyes here
for a pagan sea

Lights stand up
in a dark wood
I'm now swimming in night green
"I shall paint my body red & dance"
she said I
will wear antlers or a
bone blooded with Earth-Time
I will
I will

In sets, sets in with her
holding tight slips
Those Martian canals are
cracked ice
I cut to the Andromeda movie
"Venus" is here too
I thought my body green or faun
& dropped the sexual stick
Shadows showed the crater
to be a new moon
A story-book pomegranate split
She's got a myrtle whip
She made her name in whips
& made me worship her
Me, a mere shadow of sight
standing in the shell of the dream
eyed back into dark ovals

234

Of all the Pagans I was One
What oath is mine?
Who wouldn't bend to a
Virgin standing on the moon?
Can't resist
I'll paint myself white
You paint yourself red
We'll dance to a
Low Eastern Bright Eye tune
& follow that song
Our bedsheets will be like fire & ice
& I'll have to walk out
the next door
to close out the smell of you


THE CREATIVE IS SPEAKING It is a large you-name-it-machine made
of words to show you O Princes what's the side of He-Who-Risks
all for me, he the Bull leaper for in Bulls does the Earth-shaker
delight for in bulls does she know her truth & set down this
soft earth bed too grosse for Heaven upon which I end where
I begunne. (His loincloth will be immaculate and bright,
his bracelets will be costly, his hair curled, his face painted
red & black for a night of love)
THE CREATIVE IS SPEAKING to write a nuclear warhead, to
walk inside itself circumscribed as an obtrusive lope. The
man wants to play the music loud to think he's some kinda animal
some kinda some kind some kinda animal
Douse him or send him into the next votary's mind
He's some kind some kinda animal
Not that he's untamable but ancient you know like a
tryseerotops which is not to say it died by living
out its need

& needed more than one of us

Touched him she thought he thought
Some space between

He said about sex all over again
She said Here I go again
A couple mentions the "you" factor
you know then
She's ready too
We hold out our hearts
So what's the suffering all about?

THE CREATIVE IS SPEAKING    How the sons of immigrants go back
to fight in the ancestral homelands. Now you know you are American
Now you know how this is preserved in memory

You know how memory is cunning
That sex is early on the girl's mind
Now you know all manner of speaking openly
The myths are alive for a time
I come out full-grown out of my father's split head
and am armed for the battle of love
These words are in answer to an assignment to make sense of
3 and 5
I represented my mother back to Greece
Poo EEE Nay EEE stah sohn ton lay o for EEE on?

There is not more hope than this: to find the right bus
Athens, which is a city built on the extension of Hestia's hearth
The head split in two and something is noticed in the duality
of city life: in and out, the inner and outer working daily
for the virgin spinster who would like to make sense of all
these trade routes, know who went where when and the little
amphora handles are clues to great travelers with goods who
plunged ahead to carry with them their genetic structures
among other things, & all the manifestations of all the
senses: color, texture, taste, smell, sight

236

The spice of night
The silk of midday
The clear soup of morning
A way of studying stars
A photograph of a king
The queen's proclivities
The way people might decide on a crime & so on
On returning from Egypt I had
1 hookah
2 scarves of silk, red as my fantasy of the red in Red Sea
& 1 Mediterranean blue
1 scarab pin (imitation)
Another scarab was lost in England in the room of the lady
who said "Scarabs always get lost around me"
And from these places I brought a new appetite for a
particular olive

It was the olive branch and owl which symbolized the way men
lived before they were civilized and somewhere out of darkness
I went to meet them.


Dear Lady,

I am an ingenious amateur inventor. For five years I meditated on
trying to produce as many new good invention ideas as I could. I did
think up about 50 of them. After checking patentability I discarded
12 of them and had 38 left. When I tried to sell some to a few bus-
inessmen, I got two of them stolen. I got them witness and dis-
closure documents on the rest. I then sold one to a lady and then am
now offering any or all the 35 inventions for sale to you now. I trust
you enough to take a chance anyway. Many of these are cheap and
easy to build and make. All have good money making profit poten-
tial, some many millions profit potentially. I am not at this time
financially able to afford getting any patents because I am getting
by just barely. I hope to sell 10 or 12 of my new Inventions and then

patent two or three then myself. I did get your name from the Who's Who book in America and address. Rest easy though I'm only sending a few letters to a few ladies to try my luck and will not advertise my invention or write to any men at all about any inventions. Read the next page for more details and bless you regardless of your decision.

from Kenneth Alexander Walker

Brief Indication List of Invention Ideas of Kenneth Alexander Walker

1. Device for air improvement in homes.
2. New type of pet bird cage. Should be liked by bird lovers.
3. New type of child's tricycle.
4. New type of ladies watch band.
5. New type of stylish sun protection for eyes.
6. New type of loud noise control hearingwise.
7. New type of eyeglass frames. Should make people feel better.
8. New type of outdoor bird house. Bird lovers should like this one.
9. New type of barometer.
10. Improvement for safer night driving.
11. Burgler catcher mechanism.
12. New type of life raft.
13. Improvement for all replacement car door lock knob.
14. Method of getting massage while driving vehicle.
15. New type of food freezer. Should keep food frozen quality longer.
16. New type of refridgerator. Should keep food fresher longer.
17. New type of fish aquarium. Pet fish lovers should like.
18. New type of small animal cage for pets pet animal lovers should like.
19. New improvement for pet bird water dishes.
20. Method of improvement for men's briefcases.
21. Improvement on photo grey sun protection.
22. A camera and film picture improvement.
23. Improvement for teachers' blackboard pointers.
24. Improvement for telephone handles.
25. New type of scalp massager.
26. New type of wax candle. More light for its size compared to others.
27. Improved clothing iron women will like.
28. Light increasing lampshade electricity saver.
29. Directional light increased electricity saver.
30. Shark repelling life jacket.

31. New type of stove that is an improvement.
32. Flexibile light aimer improvement.
33. Auto window washer improvement.
34. Drinking water cooler improvement.
35. TV commercial alternative improvement.


To His Excellency Mobutu Sese Seko
    Head of State

Citoyen President:
I appeal to you for the immediate and unconditional release of
Tshisekedi wa Mulumba, a lawyer and former member of the
Zairian Assembly who was arrested last October.

I believe that Mr. wa Mulumba is a prisoner of conscience, held
solely for his nonviolent exercise of fundamental human rights.
He is reportedly held at Makala Prison in Kinshasa.

Thank you.

            Anne-Who-Grasps-The-Broom-More-Tightly


IOVIS OMNIA PLENA The world is full is full of you my lingering
one, lingam of any century of this old papa's realm of this
sweet love & sweat. Dear Father who made me so to be a poet
on the battlefield of Mars, whose seed got dipped, got used
& cannibalized to be this witness such and eke out her income
her life her light on a bed of love, earth is my is my number
O earth is the number to be joined by you old grandfather
sky and harking back to he who is the genetics to any plump
German girl, or any paranoid Huguenot daughter. I can take
him or leave him, juiced out over many wars:

                & all these messages
                   are the light
                      of me
                        the life

                 of me who receives them in the guise
of anyway you want

            hemmed in . . .

lost
willful
prepubescent in the long lunchroom hour . . .
I conquer you

A personal message:
Dearest Anne, there is so much more I wish I could say to you. This
test has been enjoyable and frustrating in equal amounts. Some-
times I wonder why I bother, but when I hear you and certain
colleagues of yours read, it at times seems worthwhile.

Looking at you, I see a romantic, an idealist, and a revolutionary.
You seem to call it the way you see it, and have no qualms about
nailing the "jello faced abominations" (My line) to the wall. You
don't have any aversion to graphically describing sexuality, pain,
life, death, the reality of what it means to be men and women.

If I seem nihilistic and cynical, it is because I am a heartbroken
utopian dreamer and romantic who has slammed up against the
grey wall of reality a considerable number of times. I live for venge-
ance, a sort of "poetic justice"

I admire how you with your greater experience of years and life
than my own can still see so much "basic goodness." But you are
still willing to call a cat a cat, a dog a dog, a man a man, and a woman
a woman. And blame few indeed for what they inherently are.

I really would like to be a successful novelist, and my audience
response at this most recent reading was better than usual, and I
got positive feedback from Rick Andy Tom. Poetry is even more
fun than drugs, you were right about that.

I got Bill Burroughs (Sr.) up on my wall smoking a joint and
looking right through you. There is beer in the fridge, Joan Ar-
matrading on the radio. Whatever you would tell me, I probably
would take it seriously.

The battle with the "Ugly spirit" is not to be discounted. Me and
my whole little faction of friends and lovers wave at you, smile, flip
the bird, blow a kiss from '77 '81 '83 '84. Here in exile I wish to know
how I can best serve all those I left behind.

Gregory Corso said something to the effect of "If you take you
shit and show it to some guy and he says THIS SUCKS you gotta say,
fuck you man, you're full of shit I'M A POET"

Burroughs said "There will be no self-pity in the ranks"

I would really like to have THE DEFINITIVE QUOTE from you. And if you want to tell me I have the whole damn thing wrong, I'll listen.

Fer-ever yours, your hopelessly sentimental and incompetent warrior in disgrace —

D.M.

D'accord that is the place to be, D'accord with him a place
to go down down on him with no music to prop this boy love

I extend to boy

It is the truth of me when I needed him and I was hard on him
& he in me, hard on me

to stay to prop this boy love
to be this fast hard boy love in me
I be it
in me, in me
to fast this love to fasten as I was hard on him to prop
his love

a violation & a forgetting      to prop all love

for I was hard on him to be a boy & love of the boy to be
a boy
go by, boy
yours in the ranks of any promise of manhood
& you are no music
you are no manhood yet

you are wonder I am spectator once      O boy!

Ye Guelfs, listen! This makes sense . . .

## Eyes in All Heads to Be Looked out Of

Formed a new beast today: eye of hawk
heart of lion, radar of bat
Crossed the psychic threshold
the same old old set of eyes
So many layers in one way of working
and you, The Other, you open every one of them
You make me exist, cold by the doorway,
chipper when we don't miss a beat,
despondent for heartbreak's sake
I am the weather when it breaks and destroys
Stroke my sleeping fur, appease me
or I'll deracinate your calm
My Other has shown his many face —
weak, selfish, you see him around woman
I am the idiot too, but will measure myself
against the most beautiful in you
and fail or not, the "I" will come out of joint
to be destroyed
I sign on the line for this thinking
of Cambodia devastated continuously by war
The lightening crackles over my head
and turns to angry pellets
Ariadne auf Naxos turns her head
to attack the aria and floats above Libyan
headlines crossing the Line of Death
Someone is waiting for me
Someone is approaching from the opposite direction
I can summon him up, I'll pull off his mask
I got this power when I wasn't looking
between two moments I fell out of
into what was like a noise, a hum
of colored seed syllables that jump on wavelengths
and charge down to the basement to the colored
rooms which only exist to think of feeding Nicaragua
I promise to light more fires till death
This is the arrogant voice of a thirsty traveler
who came through centuries to meet you
standing in the feeble posture

of the attention position
Yours in the ranks of the Phalanx appearing
now on the tarmac outside    Get in line!
Pick up the weapons: the branches & brushes,
the ankhs, the heart sutras, the wheels of time,
the precious jewels, the precious ministers,
the precious speech
The oppressed and the oppressor can meet at last
and when I heard my old poetry teacher speak
it was like the voice of rain
and I received it always in the guise of earth
Not a guise but gauze that keeps us from each other
because we are two — Me up against the world of you

Alone    Alone    Alone
Separate    Separate    Separate

Popped into this illusion to clarify speech
Into this speech, clarify speech
I'm here      I'm here
Too many eyes in one head
I see    I see    I see
I was there   I was never there
Eyes in all the heads to be looked out of
No hierarchies but natural ones, nor infinite,
Charles Olson, in the sense of eternal
No such many as mass, there are only
eyes in all the heads to be looked out of
Windows on terror, windows on lovemaking,
on any battlefield windows on the stars
The gate to the temple is a monstrous

## ROAR

I'll aim this at myself and be it a trajectory
clean to the force of things, look at
me pass under and bow

I BOW TO THE GODDESS OF TEXTURE
I BOW TO THE GODDESS OF THUNDER AND ELECTRICITY
I BOW TO THE GODDESS OF ROCK, OF CORAL
I BOW TO THE GODDESS OF DESIRE AND SELFLESS LOVE

I see this is not arguable as theory
It is refutable
But in the sense I proclaim I see      I see      I see
You can cut me back and I'll grow back on you
Not a curse, this is the way it is
Proclaiming I see  I  see      I see
And in this cutting room, cut the root

Cut root torment

Cut sorrow long way down

Cut like chill to bone           CUT

Break off all talk   CUT

Cut root thought
Cut time

Don't cling       CUT

Cut light
Cut it out
Her cutup manner slays me

Don't fixate on that one       CUT

Cut      heart

and through you and into you          CUT

I'm crazy Miss Linda Longcake
Crazy Miss Linda Longcake
Please come to a white courtesy phone

Cut one hell of a ride      C'est, ça!

Cut the fool of you, the tooth of you

The truth of you, whatever the version

Cut the need of you

The Soviet probes move on from Venus

Cut the quick of you clear of decisions

Cut defense budget, blackening oxygen

Cut historical action, personal failings

Cut tight coil of ignition of guts in abdomen

Cut ignition of guts in abdomen

Cut animal lassitude

Cut carnal money

Cut his presence, a demon to me now

& in a horse chewed voice          CUT

In the voice of a toothless hag     CUT

In the voice of "I was a girl"   CUT

In the voice of Aphrodite in arms      CUT

In the voice of one possessed       CUT

In the voice of a small one breathing
through the eye of a needle

CUT      CUT!